The Practical

# Alert! The C-Virus Pandemic Was Satan's Practice Run For A New World Order!

Roger Henri Trepanier

© 2020

Copyright 2020 © Roger Henri Trepanier

Scripture taken from

THE NEW AMERICAN STANDARD BIBLE ®, Copyright © 1960, 1962, 1963, 1968, 1971, 1972, 1973, 1975, 1977, 1995 by The Lockman Foundation. Used by permission.

This book is available for purchase in print format or as an eBook on all major distribution channels

The author may be contacted at the website:

http://www.pilgrimpathwaypublications.com

**Trademarks:**

Pilgrim Pathway Publications™, Servant of God Most High™, The Truth Seeker's Library™, The Practical Helps Library™, The Christian Fiction Library™, and The Word Of God Library™ are trademarks of Roger Henri Trepanier

**All Rights Reserved**

No part of this book may be reproduced in any form without permission in writing from the author. An exception is granted to a reviewer who wishes to quote a brief passage or two as part of a public review of this book.

This book is dedicated to all my brothers and sisters who are also believers in God's Son, The Lord Jesus Christ. May we all constantly be aware, in these dark and last days, that our time of glorification could occur at any time, and until that moment comes, the task for which we are still here has still not be completed! So let us all keep in mind God's charge to all of us through His Son at Matthew 28:19,20:

"Go therefore and make disciples of all the nations, baptizing them in the name of the Father and the Son and the Holy Spirit, teaching them to observe all that I commanded you; and lo, I am with you always, even to the end of the age."

## Titles available from Roger Henri Trepanier in The Truth Seeker's Library™ series:

God Did Not Create Human Beings To Die… But To Live On… Eternally!
Finding Comfort And Encouragement In The Promises Of God In The Last Days
How We Know For Sure That We Are Living In The Last Days!
Have You Ever Wondered What Happens After Death?
An Introduction To The New World That Is Coming On The Earth
Deeper Truths Of The Christian Life
Evangelism As God Intended
Keeping On Serving God In The Last Days
The Mysterious World Of Angels And Demons
No One Loves As He Loves!
Thanks Be To God For His Indescribable Gift!
The Church Is Very Much Alive, Well, And Growing!
Tracing The Steps Of The Son Of God From Eternity To Eternity!
War, And Going To War, Is Simply Not Of God!
God Never Meant Prayer To Be A Mystery!
Health Is One Of God's Great Blessings!
Removing The Mystery Surrounding Baptism!
This World's Return To Paganism Is Almost Complete!
Removing The Mystery Surrounding Heaven!
God's Covenants Were Meant For Mankind's Blessing!
The Four Ages Of Time
The Awesomeness Of God!

## Titles available from Roger Henri Trepanier in The Practical Helps Library™ series:

Learning to Overcome The Perplexities Of This Present Life
So, I Hear You Want To Work With Seniors?
I Will Not Have This Man To Rule Over Me!
Spiritual Truth To Warm The Heart!
Fasten Your Seatbelts: Turbulence Ahead!
Living A Normal Christian Life In An Increasingly Abnormal World!
If You Have Jesus; You Do Not Need Drugs!
To Do God's Will Is To Have A Foretaste Of Heaven!
This World Is Ready For The Rule Of The Antichrist!

President Trump And The Q Movement Versus Satan And The Deep State
More Of God's Great Promises For Comfort And Encouragement!

## Titles available from Roger Henri Trepanier in The Christian Fiction Library™ series:

The Beginning Of A New Dawn
It Is Never Too Late For Love!
The True To Life Musings Of Fred And Ernie
Between A Rock And A Hard Place!
Love Knows No Boundaries!
A Woman Worth Pursuing!
Love Is More Than Just A Four Letter Word!
The Twists And Turns Of The Life Of Faith!

## Titles available from Roger Henri Trepanier in The Word Of God Library™ series:

God's First Letter To The Thessalonians
God's Second Letter To The Thessalonians
God's Letter To Believers Through Jude
God's Three Short Letters To Believers Through John
God's Letter To Scattered Believers Through James
God's Letter To Titus
God's Prophetic Word To Mankind Through Daniel
God's Letter To Philemon And God's Letter To The Colossians
God's Consummation Of All In The Book Of Revelation
God's Letter To The Philippians
God's First Letter Through Peter

# INTRODUCTION

Never in the history of the world – and not even during two world wars – have we seen such fear and panic grip one nation after another, leading not only to the shutdown of the world economy, but to all activities except essential services! In country after country, businesses were shut down and people told to stay indoors as much as possible, only going out for food and supplies! Never in the history of the world have people been called to practice social distancing or to wear a mask when one did go out, with people actually being arrested and fined if they did not! Never in the history of the world have we seen authorities enact such draconian measures on their people, such as keeping track of their every movement by way of their smartphone, and by way of drones equipped with cameras, face recognition, and loudspeakers to warn people! Never in the history of the world have we seen such a trampling of human rights on a global scale, from the removal of the freedom of movement to that of gathering, and even of expression!

From the moment the director of WHO (World Health Organization) announced that the coronavirus had become a pandemic on March 11, 2020, my reaction was: You have to be kidding me, right? Even by that date it was well-known by those who follow alternative media – and not the mainstream media – that this viral outbreak, which began a few months earlier in Wuhan, China, was not even as serious as the yearly seasonal flu! So the question immediately arose in my mind, and no doubt in the mind of many others also: Why was this declared a pandemic then?

What made matters worse is that this virus came out of China – as have many viruses of recent memory – which is a Communist-led country, which means that any information they share is immediately suspect, since it is not in their best interest to ever tell the truth! So, what this Communist government did not share with the world – with this information only becoming known as this virus came to more open societies – is that the vast majority of those dying from this virus were the elderly, with almost all having at least one underlying pre-condition that made them susceptible to dying in the first place!

What this book's central focus will be then is to show that behind this C- virus pandemic, there was a dark agenda at work, fueled by Deep

State entities – such as the United Nations, Bill Gates, the main stream media, Big Pharma, the Democratic party, and many more – and behind the curtain as unseen was an even more sinister and far deadlier foe, which is Satan, the devil. What this means then is that this pandemic was just a front for a deeper agenda than just the immediate goal of crashing the US economy and stopping President Trump from being re-elected in 2020!

For what needs to be grasped is that Satan's ultimate agenda is to bring in a one world government and a one world religion so that he can bring to this earth his own counterfeits to the Trinity, that being Satan himself counterfeiting God The Father, the antichrist counterfeiting God's Son, and the false prophet counterfeiting The Holy Spirit! So, what this book will do then is to give evidence of how the devil did use this C-virus pandemic as an attempt at bringing in a new world order with his counterfeits at the elm, as assisted by the Deep State of this present world system!

Then as to the arrangement of the book itself, we are to note that it has been divided into three sections. The first section deals with Satan, the devil; and with the Deep State; the second section deals with this C-virus pandemic and especially relating to how it has been used by Satan as a practice run for his one world government; and then the third section deals with how God has so far used President Trump and his administration, plus Q and the Q movement, and the believers of this earth to hold back Satan's agenda on earth! And the reason that we need to begin with Satan, and then look at the Deep State before we look at this pandemic is due to the fact that we need to have a firm grasp of the devils' agenda before we can then grasp how he has used the Deep State to further his agenda through this pandemic.

Then we are to note that at the back of the book there is an Addenda with four sections. In Addendum A, there is a brief outline of the four ages of time, for any reading this book who might not be aware of the fact that God has divided all of time into four ages. Then in Addendum B, there is a brief outline of the two comings from Heaven to earth in time of God's Son, The Lord Jesus Christ, for any who may not be familiar with this information either. In Addendum C, we have a presentation of the gospel, which is the good news that God gives in His word regarding His Son, The Lord Jesus Christ, for any readers who might not as yet have that vital personal relationship with God through faith in His Son. And then in Addendum D, under 'Useful resources,' we have important information regarding the video and article links referenced in this book. It is recommended that one start with the Addenda before reading the book proper.

And before closing this Introduction, we should mention a few things of a personal nature, since we are all somewhat curious human beings. So after completing 21 years of formal education and then spending almost 28 years working in Project Engineering and Management in the Corporate offices of a couple of large utilities, God called His servant as a non-denominational evangelist in early 1999, and then sent him out more than two thousand miles away from family and friends, to the place of service God has assigned, which is where His servant has been, and is still serving Him, as evangelist, counselor, and author. God's servant is a widower with three adopted children, all now married with a family of their own.

Please note the two websites listed below, which have been established for the purpose of interacting with readers and also for gospel ministry:

http://www.pilgrimpathwaypublications.com

http://servantofmosthigh.com

And now my prayer is that God will richly bless you as you read this book, and greatly minister to every need in your life, as only God can! To Him be all praise, honor, and glory, with thanksgiving, both now and forevermore! Amen.

# CONTENTS

Page

Introduction

Alert! The C-Virus Pandemic Was Satan's Practice Run For A New World Order!

| | | |
|---|---|---|
| **SECTION ONE** | **SATAN: WHO HE IS, HIS MAIN EVIL CHARACTER TRAITS, HIS AGENDA, AND THE DEEP STATE AS HIS USEFUL TOOL** | |
| Chapter One | Who Satan is | 17 |
| Chapter Two | Satan's main character traits | 23 |
| Chapter Three | Satan's evil agenda | 31 |
| Chapter Four | The deep state, as Satan's useful tool | 45 |
| **SECTION TWO** | **SEEING THE C-Virus PANDEMIC AS THE OUTWORKING OF SATAN'S AGENDA BY WAY OF THE DEEP STATE** | |
| Chapter Five | Five reasons why the C-virus outbreak should never have been called as a pandemic! | 61 |
| Chapter Six | How Satan has furthered his agenda through the C-virus pandemic, as assisted by the Deep State | 71 |
| Chapter Seven | How Satan has used the C-virus pandemic and the Deep State to weaken and seek to eliminate the foundations that God established for stable societies | 79 |
| **SECTION THREE** | **PRESIDENT TRUMP, Q, BELIEVERS, AND GOD ACTING TO RESTRAIN SATAN IN CARRYING OUT HIS AGENDA** | |
| Chapter Eight | President Trump and his administration | 91 |
| Chapter Nine | Q and the Q movement worldwide | 97 |

"Then He will also say to those on His left, 'Depart from Me, accursed ones, into the eternal fire which has been prepared for the devil and his angels."

Matthew 25:41

# CHAPTER ONE

## Who Satan is

Before we can speak of who Satan is, we need to begin with when creation took place (Genesis 1:1), which was also when time began to be marked (Genesis 1:14-16). At that point in time, God was in the process of bringing into existence all that presently exists in the universe, of what can be seen and what is unseen, doing so through His six days of creation. And before God rested on the seventh day (Genesis 2:1-3), He declared at Genesis 1:31, regarding His creation just brought into existence, "God saw all that He had made, and behold, it was very good. And there was evening and there was morning, the sixth day."

What this means then, when God says, "it was very good," is that human and angelic beings had been created and were all sinless. In other words, there was no sin in all creation, and therefore no evil, in that no sin had yet taken place among humans or among the angelic beings. Unfortunately, that was about to change, which would eventually affect the eternal destiny of a third of the human race and a third of the angelic beings!

For what we now need to observe is that when we come to Genesis 3:1, we are introduced to a serpent, who now comes and leads Adam and Eve into sin, with their subsequent loss of innocence through that sin. However, what concerns us here is not the sin of Adam and Eve (which was disobedience to God's command on Adam's part, noting Genesis 2:15-17 and pride on Eve's part, noting Genesis 3:1-6), but rather that of the serpent, which God identifies for us at Revelation 12:9 as follows, "And the great dragon was thrown down, THE SERPENT OF OLD WHO IS CALLED THE DEVIL AND SATAN, who deceives the whole world; he was thrown down to the earth, and his angels were thrown down with him."

Since Satan, the devil, had already sinned against God by Genesis 3:1, when he tempted Adam and Eve to sin, and since at the end of Genesis 1 we have seen that God declared all of His creation to be "very good," then this means that Satan had to himself sin against God at some point after Genesis 1:31 and before Genesis 3:1, when he came to lead our first parents, Adam and Eve, into sin. So, when did that occur?

Since the whole of God's word is concerned with mankind as the pinnacle of God's creation, since created in His image (noting Genesis 1:26), then this means that whatever we are told by God about the angelic beings is what we learn indirectly from God's word, where God's main focus is His dealings with mankind over the millennia and centuries. And so, one passage that has come to be ascribed to God speaking of Satan's fall into sin by Biblical scholars is what we read at Isaiah 14:12-15 for instance, "[12] How you have fallen from heaven, O star of the morning, son of the dawn! You have been cut down to the earth, You who have weakened the nations! [13] But you said in your heart, 'I will ascend to heaven; I will raise my throne above the stars of God, and I will sit on the mount of assembly in the recesses of the north. [14] I will ascend above the heights of the clouds; I will make myself like the Most High.' [15] Nevertheless you will be thrust down to Sheol, to the recesses of the pit."

There are a number of things we learn about Satan, the devil, from this passage. We see that he went from being in heaven to the pit, that is, from God's own uncreated and eternally existing dwelling to the lowest place below the surface of this present earth, due to being filled with pride, for in his heart, after his sinless creation by God, he wanted to not only be "like the Most High," but actually occupy the place above God Himself, in that he said, "I will raise my throne above the stars of God," which are the angelic beings in God's Presence here (noting Revelation 1:20). So what we learn here about Satan, the devil, is that he sinned due to pride, with his desire then being to rule in the place of God!

A second passage of God's word, where God indirectly tells us about Satan, the devil, is at Ezekiel 28:12-17, where we see God begin by speaking to the prophet Ezekiel here, as "the son of man", with God then leading him to write down what then follows, "[12] Son of man, take up a lamentation over the king of Tyre and say to him, 'Thus says the Lord God, "You had the seal of perfection, full of wisdom and perfect in beauty. 13] You were in Eden, the garden of God; every precious stone was your covering: The ruby, the topaz and the diamond; the beryl, the onyx and the jasper; the lapis lazuli, the turquoise and the emerald; and the gold, the workmanship of your settings and sockets, was in you. On the day that you were created they were prepared. [14] You were the anointed cherub who covers, and I placed you there. You were on the holy mountain of God; You walked in the midst of the stones of fire. [15] You were blameless in your ways from the day you were created until unrighteousness was found in you. [16] By the abundance of your trade you were internally filled with violence, and you sinned; therefore I have cast you as profane from the mountain of God. and I have destroyed you (speaking of loss of wellbeing, not of being), O covering cherub, from the midst of the stones of fire. [17] Your heart was lifted up because of your beauty; you corrupted your wisdom by reason of your splendor. I cast you to the ground; I put you before kings, that they may see you."

And what we further learn about Satan, the devil, from this passage of God's word is that he was created by God as a sinless cherub, which is an order of angelic beings, and at some point after that he sinned against God (verse 15, "You were blameless in your ways from the day you were created until unrighteousness was found in you"), with his fall being due to the sin of pride (verse 17, "Your heart was lifted up because of your beauty; you corrupted your wisdom by reason of your splendor").

Therefore, based on the information we have looked at from God's word in this chapter so far, we can say the following about Satan, the devil: 1) he was created by God as a sinless cherub; 2) he sinned against God due to pride; 3) that sin due to pride occurred at some time after Genesis 1:31 and before Genesis 3:1; 4) he had the goal of not only being like God, but of actually ruling instead of God; 5) he is seen to have led Adam and Eve into sin, which means he also introduced evil and death to the human race (Romans 5:12); and 6) he is the leader over angels, which he also led into rebellion against God (Revelation 12:9, "his angels").

"the one who practices sin is of the devil; for the devil has sinned from the beginning. The Son of God appeared for this purpose, to destroy the works of the devil."

1 John 3:8

# CHAPTER TWO

## Satan's main evil character traits

What we now want to do in this second chapter is go deeper into the evil character of this fallen angelic being, whom God refers to as Satan, the devil. And here we will look at just five of his main character traits, these being as a murderer, a liar, a deceiver, a tempter, and a counterfeiter!

*Satan is a murderer and a liar*

And so, to begin with here, let us note what God's Son, The Lord Jesus Christ, told unbelievers of His day at John 8:44 about this evil entity, "You are of your father the devil, and you want to do the desires of your father. He was a murderer from the beginning, and does not stand in the truth because there is no truth in him. Whenever he speaks a lie, he speaks from his own nature, for he is a liar and the father of lies."

Here we have two very important pieces of information regarding Satan, the devil, which are: 1) he is a murderer, which is from the beginning; and 2) he is a liar and the father of lies! And to help us understand this further, we are to realize that when God says he was a murderer from the beginning, God refers to the fact that it was the devil who not only introduced sin into the human race, as we see at Genesis 3:6, but it was also the devil who introduced murder into the human race also!

We know this because at Genesis 4:8 we read the following (in part), "And it came about when they were in the field, that Cain rose up against Abel his brother and killed him, " with God then commenting on this at 1 John 3:11,12, there saying, "For this is the message which you have heard from the beginning, that we should love one another; not as CAIN, WHO WAS OF THE EVIL ONE and slew his brother. And for what reason did he slay him? Because his deeds were evil, and his brother's were righteous."

So here we see that the first murder to occur in the human race in time was through an unbeliever, Cain, who acting as a tool of the devil killed Abel, who was a believer, that is, one who had a personal relationship with God. This is important to remember as we continue!

Then secondly, from John 8:44 quoted above, God's Son also told us that the devil was "a liar and the father of lies." So, what this tells us is that whenever we see someone lie, then we can be absolutely sure that the person is being a tool of the devil in doing so! In other words, all lies have their source with the devil, same as all truth has its source in God and is found in God's word (Psalm 119:160; John 17:17).

*Satan is a deceiver*

As we continue, let us note again what God says at Revelation 12:9, about Satan, the devil, "And the great dragon was thrown down, the serpent of old who is called the devil and Satan, who deceives the whole world; he was thrown down to the earth, and his angels were thrown down with him." What we are to further see here is that all lies are a form of deception, in that it is an attempt to keep another person from discovering or knowing the truth! And so, when God tells us at Revelation 12:9 above that the devil "deceives the whole world," then we are to keep in mind that this is done through lies, whether that be through an outright lie, disinformation, half-truths, or fake news! This is also important for us to remember as we go on.

*Satan is a tempter*

Let us note another major evil character trait of Satan, which is as tempter. When Satan, the devil, came to Adam and Eve in the form of a serpent at Genesis 3:1, it was to tempt them to sin, by deceiving Eve into believing a lie, resulting in her doing the devil's bidding, instead of obeying the command that God had already given Adam to obey at Genesis 2:16. So what we are to remember then is that Satan often combines some of his evil character traits, doing whatever is necessary in order to get human beings to do his bidding instead of God's will.

So let us note that interchange between Satan as the serpent and Eve at Genesis 3:1-6, adding comments in brackets as a help, "[1] Now the serpent was more crafty than any beast of the field which the Lord God had made. And he said to the woman, "Indeed, has God said (raises doubt in Eve's mind), 'You shall not eat from any tree of the garden'?" [2] The woman said to the serpent, "From the fruit of the trees of the garden we may eat; [3] but from the fruit of the tree which is in the middle of the garden, God has said, 'You shall not eat from it or touch it, or you will die.' " [4] The serpent said to the woman, "You surely will not die! (Satan here tells Eve an outright lie) [5] For God knows that in the day you eat from it your eyes will be opened, and you will be like God, knowing good and evil" (Satan deceiving Eve through another lie, tempting Eve with a seemingly better way than God) [6] When the woman saw that the tree (that God had forbidden them to eat from) was good for food (this was greed, as God had provided all that was good in the other trees also there for food), and that it was a delight to the eyes (lusting after something that God had forbidden), and that the tree was desirable to make one wise (this was pride, not being satisfied with God's endowment of them at creation), she took from its fruit and ate; and she gave also to her husband with her, and he ate."

And so, what we should be aware of here is that the devil has three key sins that he likes to use to tempt the whole of the human race, and so keep them in bondage to him, with these three sins being: lust (that is, desires that are not of God), greed, and pride. One passage where God makes us aware of these three sins is at 1 John 2:16, where we read, "For all that is in the world, the lust of the flesh (the desire for what is not of God) and the lust of the eyes (greed) and the boastful pride of life, is not from the Father, but is from the world," with "the world" that God mentions here presently being under Satan's control, as is clear from 1 John 5:19, "We know that we (believers) are of God, and that the whole world lies in the power of the evil one" (Satan).

And what is really interesting to note here, before going further, is that these three sins, namely, pride, greed, and lust, are the exact same three sins that Satan, as the serpent of old, did use to also tempt God's precious Son with, The Lord Jesus Christ, at the start of His public ministry, noting what we read at Matthew 4:1-11, with comments in brackets as a help, [1] Then Jesus was led up by the Spirit into the wilderness to be tempted by the devil. [2] And after He had fasted forty days and forty nights, He then became hungry. [3] And the tempter came and said to Him, "If You are the Son of God (tries to introduce doubt, same as with Eve), command that these stones become bread" (tempting to greed) [4] But He answered and said, "It is written, 'Man shall not live on bread alone, but on every word that proceeds out of the mouth of God.' " [5] Then the devil took Him into the holy city and had Him stand on the pinnacle of the temple, [6] and said to Him, "If You are the Son of God, throw Yourself down; for it is written, 'He will command His angels concerning You'; And 'On their hands they will bear You up, so that You will not strike Your foot against a stone' " (God's Son being tempted by lust here, with a desire to experience something out of His Father's will for Him to do). [7] Jesus said to him, "On the other hand, it is written, 'You shall not put the Lord your God to the test.' " [8] Again, the devil took Him to a very high mountain and showed Him all the kingdoms of the world and their glory; [9] and he said to Him, "All these things I will give You, if You fall down and worship me" (which was to tempt God's Son with pride, offering something that was not God His Father's will for Him at this time). [10] Then Jesus said to him, "Go, Satan! For it is written, 'You shall worship the Lord your God, and serve Him only.' " [11] Then the devil left Him; and behold, angels came and began to minister to Him."

And so, we see here that God's Son was victorious over each one of the devil's three temptations, the same three that Adam and Eve fell to at the beginning, being the same three that the devil does tempt the human race with down to our day. What we are to grasp here also is that God's Son had come from Heaven to earth to undo the devil's work (1 John 3:8) and was on His way to the cross, where all the devil's work would be undone, namely of his having brought sin and death to the human race!

So that process of undoing all the devil's work started when God's Son died on the cross, bearing there the sins of a sinful human race (1 Peter 3:18), he was buried to put those sins away, then raised from the dead the third day to be alive forever, thereby providing His Father with a basis for forgiving the sins and bestowing eternal life to any human being who comes to God by faith in Him! And that process will be completed when God raises all believers and unbelievers from the dead one day.

*Satan is a counterfeiter*

As we continue looking at Satan's main evil character traits, let us note what God tells us at 2 Corinthians 11:13-15, "[13] For such men are false apostles, deceitful workers, disguising themselves as apostles of Christ. [14] No wonder, for even Satan disguises himself as an angel of light. [15] Therefore it is not surprising if his servants also disguise themselves as servants of righteousness, whose end will be according to their deeds." What this means then is that we should not expect Satan to come to us in a recognizable way – and certainly not with a tail, horns, and a pitch fork – but always in a way that will be seen as an attempt to deceive us to accept the counterfeit, instead of what is real! We will have more to say about Satan's counterfeiting scheme in the next chapter, when we look at his agenda that he is seeking to outwork.

"And the devil who deceived them was thrown into the lake of fire and brimstone, where the beast and the false prophet are also; and they will be tormented day and night forever and ever."

Revelation 20:10

# CHAPTER THREE

## Satan's evil agenda

We have already seen from the first chapter that Satan's goal from the beginning was not only to be like God, but to actually rule the world instead of God! And now in this chapter, we are to see how Satan plans to carry out his agenda through time. And what we are to grasp from the outset is that the devil's principal method of accomplishing his agenda of not only opposing all that God does, but also to counterfeit all that God is doing!

*A Satan-inspired false religious system*

So the first thing that Satan did at the beginning, after leading the human race into sin, was to establish through the first unbeliever, Cain, a Satan-inspired false religious system on earth, to counter the true religious system that God had already established through Adam, which was then also practiced by his brother Abel and their believing descendants. This true religion was based on God having made known at Genesis 3:15 with Genesis 3:22 that His Son was coming to earth one day, as born of a woman, to die in the place of guilty sinners, which was foreshadowed until He came through the animal sacrifices and offerings that God introduced to mankind. And so, whoever believed in God's Son to come, would be receiving the forgiveness of sins and eternal life with God. For us now, we look back at the death of God's Son at the cross, His burial, and His resurrection from the dead the third day, and believing that God's Son did this for us personally, then we too receive the forgiveness of sins and eternal life with God (noting 1 Corinthians 15:1-4).

And so, to counter this knowledge of how to have a personal relationship with God through faith in God's Son for salvation, the devil introduced a system of religion, which was based on one's own good works. We see this clearly at Genesis 4:3-5,8, "[3] So it came about in the course of time that Cain brought an offering to the Lord of the fruit of the ground. [4] Abel, on his part also brought of the firstlings of his flock and of their fat portions. and the Lord had regard for Abel and for his offering; [5] but for Cain and for his offering he had no regard. So Cain became very angry and his countenance fell…[8] And it came about when they were in the field, that Cain rose up against Abel his brother and killed him."

Let us ask two very pertinent questions here. The first question is: Why did God accept Abel's offering to Him, but did not accept Cain's offering? And then the second question is: Why did Cain kill his brother Abel? What is instructive here is to see that God Himself gives the answer to both questions later in His word, noting again what we read at 1 John 3:11,12, "[11] For this is the message which you (as believers) have heard from the beginning (noting John 13:35), that we should love one another; [12] not as CAIN, WHO WAS OF THE EVIL ONE AND SLEW HIS BROTHER. And for what reason did he slay him? Because his deeds were evil, and his brother's were righteous."

Here we see that God says Cain killed Abel because he "was of the evil one" (noting again John 8:44). And let us also note here what God says of Cain and Abel at verse 12, "his deeds were evil, and his brother's were righteous." In other words, Cain was an unbeliever rendering service to the devil, while Abel was a believer rendering service to God! We need to realize here that Adam would have shared the knowledge of salvation with both his sons, which resulted in Abel placing his faith in God's coming Son, which was why he offered God a sacrifice of an innocent animal, which God did accept, because he was showing by this that he believed in God's coming Son; while Cain rejected God's message of salvation, which is why he did not bring to God an offering of an innocent animal in sacrifice, and why God did not accept his offering!

What we are to grasp from this is that we see the devil here having established a false religious system on earth through Cain, which meant that God's plan of salvation was rejected, and instead A

SATAN-INSPIRITED RELIGION WAS ESTABLISHED, WHERE MAN IN UNBELIEF SOUGHT TO BE RIGHT WITH GOD THROUGH ONE'S OWN WORKS! In other words, man's way was to bypass God's plan of salvation and substitute one's own, which is to think that what man provides will be adequate and acceptable to God. And so, right up to our present day, all false religious systems of men on earth, which God did not institute, all have as their basis this false teaching that my good deeds or works will get me right with God, and then into Heaven one day, no matter what that 'Heaven' might be conceived to be. God warns mankind in unbelief in His word at Proverbs 14:12, "There is a way which seems right to a man, but its end is the way of death."

Then after Satan introduced that false religious system on earth, he kept seeking to keep human beings from knowing the truth of God, and so be saved, by using his usual tools, which are lies through deception, and murder, through either single acts of violence and on a mass scale through wars, plus the sins of lust, greed, and pride, all the while convincing the human race that their good works were enough to get them into heaven one day; lies and tools that have carried on over centuries and thousands of years even unto our own day!

*Satan's counterfeits: the devil, the antichrist, and the false prophet*

However, since the devil's agenda consists of also ruling in the place of God, we now need to see how Satan, the devil, plans to accomplish this. And in order to grasp this, we need to see that it is again through counterfeiting what God does. In other words, since God has made Himself known as One God in Three Persons, namely The Father, The Son, and The Holy Spirit, then Satan plans on bringing to earth His own counterfeits, with himself as replacing God The Father, the antichrist to replace God's Son, The Lord Jesus Christ; and the false prophet, to replace The Holy Spirit!

So let us first note that God did point to an 'antichrist' as coming on the world scene from what He made known in His word at 1 John 2:18, "Children, it is the last hour; and just as you heard that antichrist is coming, even now many antichrists have appeared; from this we know that it is the last hour." Let us notice three important facts from what God tells us here, with the first being that there is a person known as "antichrist" that "is coming."

Then secondly, let us notice that God says, "even now many antichrists have appeared." And what is very important to grasp from this is that God is saying that there are many people during this present third age of time who could be characterized as "antichrists," simply because they are not only displaying the same evil character traits that devil has, and that the antichrist himself will also have when he comes on the world scene, but these people are actually, knowingly or unknowingly, preparing this world for his coming! Then the third fact we need to grasp is that whenever this second truth is seen, as being a reality in the world, then we are to know that "it is the last hour" of the present third age of time, and so we need to be prepared for this present age will soon be ending!

And one reason for looking at the antichrist here is not only because it is part of the devil's work on earth in time, but it is also to help believers have their eyes open to what is going on at the present time, for the simple reason that when the antichrist comes on the world scene, IT WILL BE TO A WORLD THAT HAS ALREADY BEEN PREPARED FOR HIM! In other words, this world will have been prepared by the devil for unbelievers to not only accept the antichrist, but to also be willing to serve him as ruling over a one world government when he comes! What this means then, as was noted above from 1 John 2:18, is that the EVIL CHARACTER TRAITS the antichrist will have when he comes will very much be present among the unbelievers of this world, as the present third age of time comes to a close!

And what would be instructive for us to do now is to note what God says about when the antichrist will be on earth, which is during a seven year period immediately after the end of the present third age of time, which will be the last seven years remaining of the second age of time. And there are two passages of God's word that we specifically want to focus on here, which are 2 Thessalonians 2:1-12, followed by Revelation 13:1-18. In both these passages we will see that the EVIL CHARACTER TRAITS that the antichrist displays during this seven-year period are the same evil character traits that are now being seen among the unbelievers of earth in these last days of the present third age of time!

And so, let us now look at what God specifically says regarding the antichrist at 2 Thessalonians 2, where we will look at verses 1 to 12 for context, and again include some comments in brackets as a help, "[1] Now we request you, brethren, with regard to the coming of our Lord Jesus Christ (in the first phase of His second coming, which is at the end of the present third age of time) and our gathering together to Him (being when the believers of the present third age, who have died or who are yet alive, are now seen to be taken from the earth to Heaven, as we see at 1 Thessalonians 4:14-17), [2] that you not be quickly shaken from your composure or be disturbed either by a spirit or a message or a letter as if from us, to the effect that the day of the Lord has come (with this "day of The Lord" in this case being in reference to the seven year period during which the antichrist will be on earth). [3] Let no one in any way deceive you, for it (the day of The Lord) will not come unless the apostasy comes first, and the man of lawlessness is revealed, the son of destruction (in reference to the antichrist in these two terms), [4] who opposes and exalts himself above every so-called god or object of worship, so that he takes his seat in the temple of God, displaying himself as being God. [5] Do you not remember that while I was still with you, I was telling you these things? [6] And you know what restrains him now, so that in his time he (the antichrist) will be revealed. [7] For the mystery of lawlessness is already at work (during this present third age of time); only he (in reference to The Holy Spirit indwelling believers on earth during the present age) who now restrains will do so until he is taken out of the way (when The Holy Spirit is removed from the earth by God, along with all the believers of this present third age, as we see at 1 Thessalonians 4:14-17, then the antichrist will be revealed here on earth, as is clear from the next verse). [8] Then that lawless one (the antichrist) will be revealed whom the Lord (God's Son) will slay with the breath of His mouth and bring to an end by the appearance of His coming (which is now the second stage of His second coming and is at the end of the seven year period, as we see at Revelation 19:11-21); [9] that is, the one (the antichrist) whose coming is in accord with the activity of Satan, with all power and signs and false wonders, [10] and with all the deception of wickedness for those who perish, because they (the unbelievers of the present third age) did not receive the love of the truth so as to be saved. [11] For this reason God will send upon them (the unbelievers) a deluding influence so that they will believe what is false (because already totally conditioned to believe lies, such as fake news!), [12] in order that they all may be judged who did not believe the truth, but took pleasure in wickedness."

And now let us go on here to note the most prominent evil character traits of the antichrist from the passage above, which we must remember will be apparent in the unbelievers as this present third age comes to an end. And the first character trait that we need to notice here is that the antichrist will not only display an open hatred of God and of believers, but will also put himself forth as God and will seek to destroy the unbelievers of earth. Then secondly, which follows from this, is that the antichrist will openly, knowingly, and willingly be serving Satan, the devil. Thirdly, the antichrist will be, as "the man of lawlessness," in total disregard of the laws governing mankind on earth, which are generally derived from God's word; but he will instead be a law unto himself!

Then fourthly, we are to see that the antichrist, as "the son of destruction," will have no regard at all for the sanctity of human life, so that he is willing to be violent and kill without restraint all who oppose! And a fifth evil character trait is to display nothing but deception and lies; with a sixth being that he shows no restraint whatsoever in blaspheming God and what pertains to Him; with a seventh one being to note here that he will gladly be taking his seat and rule over a one world government with total control of all those on earth, believers and unbelievers alike! So, as we see here, what awaits us in the days ahead in not a pretty picture, which is why believers in particular need to have their eyes wide open!

So now, let us go on and look at the course of this seven-year rule of the antichrist during the last seven years remaining of the second age of time, which God gives us a picture of at Revelation 6:1 to Revelation 19:21 in His word. In other words, in this portion of God's word we have a God-given outline of what transpires on earth during those seven years under the rule of the antichrist. But since we cannot look at this whole portion here, since it would be beyond the scope of this book, let us look only at Revelation 13, where God gives us microscopic view of that same seven period, and where we clearly see the rule of the antichrist, assisted by the false prophet, and let us note again the evil character traits that these counterfeits of Satan will have.

And so, let us quote Revelation 13:1-18 in its entirety here, with some notes added in brackets as a help, before we then comment in brief on portions that pertain specifically to our present subject, "[1] And the dragon (who is Satan, the devil, noting Revelation 12:9) stood on the sand of the seashore. Then I saw a beast (the antichrist) coming up out of the sea (nations), having ten horns and seven heads, and on his horns were ten diadems, and on his heads were blasphemous names. [2] And the beast (as the antichrist) which I saw was like a leopard, and his feet were like those of a bear, and his mouth like the mouth of a lion. And the dragon (the devil) gave him his power and his throne and great authority. [3] I saw one of his heads as if it had been slain, and his fatal wound was healed. And the whole earth was amazed and followed after the beast (the antichrist); [4] they worshiped the dragon (the devil) because he gave his authority to the beast (the antichrist); and they (all unbelievers of earth) worshiped the beast (the antichrist), saying, "Who is like the beast (the antichrist), and who is able to wage war with him?" [5] There was given to him a mouth speaking arrogant words and blasphemies, and authority to act for forty-two months (which has in view here the first three and half years of the seven year period) was given to him. [6] And he opened his mouth in blasphemies against God, to blaspheme His name and His tabernacle, that is, those who dwell in heaven. [7] It was also given to him to make war with the saints (the believers whom God will have saved at the beginning of the seven years) and to overcome them, and authority over every tribe and people and tongue and nation was given to him (thereby seeing that it is a worldwide rule). [8] All who dwell on the earth will worship him, everyone whose name has not been written from the foundation of the world in the book of life of the Lamb who has been slain (which means ALL unbelievers will worship the antichrist, bar none). [9] If anyone has an ear, let him hear. [10] If anyone is destined for captivity, to captivity he goes; if anyone kills with the sword, with the sword he must be killed. Here is the perseverance and the faith of the saints (believers). [11] Then I saw another beast (the false prophet, noting Revelation 19:20) coming up out of the earth; and he had two horns like a lamb and he spoke as a dragon. [12] He exercises all the authority of the first beast (the antichrist) in his presence (in other words, while the antichrist is the political leader during those seven years, the false prophet will be the religious leader of the false world religion, that is devil-derived and inspired, and he will be focused in serving under the antichrist during the last three and half years of that seven year period). And he (the false prophet) makes the earth and those who dwell in it to worship the first beast (the antichrist), whose fatal wound was healed. [13] He (the false prophet) performs great signs, so that he even makes fire come down out of heaven to the earth in the presence of men. [14] And he deceives (just the unbelievers of) those who dwell on the earth because of the signs which it was given him to perform in the presence of the beast (the antichrist), telling (the unbelievers of) those who dwell on the earth to make an image to the beast (the antichrist) who had the wound of the sword and has come to life. [15] And it was given to him (the false prophet) to give breath to the image of the beast (the antichrist), so that the image of the beast would even speak and cause as many as do not worship the image of the beast to be killed. [16] And he (the false prophet) causes all, the small and the great, and the rich and the poor, and the free men and the slaves, to be given a mark on their right hand or on their forehead (which only the unbelievers will take), [17] and he provides that no one will be able to buy or to sell, except the one who has the mark, either the name of the beast (the antichrist) or the number of his name. [18] Here is wisdom. Let him who has understanding calculate the number of the beast (the antichrist), for the number is that of a man; and his number is six hundred and sixty-six" (666).

The first comment we need to make here is that we see three evil entities being introduced to us by God, that being the dragon at verse 13:1, who is the devil; then the first beast also at verse 13:1, who is the antichrist; and finally the second beast introduced at verse 13:11, who is the false prophet. And it is clear from the end of verse 13:2 that the antichrist is under the devil's direct power and authority and sits on the devil's throne visibly while on earth. In other words, the antichrist, as the political leader, is ruling over a one world government, which takes in all the nations of the earth, as is clear from the end of verse 13:7, doing so visibly on behalf of the devil, who is unseen. And then the false prophet, as the leader of the devil's false religious system of earth, assists the antichrist, which is during the last three and a half years, which is when he comes on the scene.

The import of what has just been mentioned is that this evil trio are not human beings per se, but rather fallen angels! In other words, we know that the devil is Satan, a cherub, which is an order of angelic beings. What this means here then is that the antichrist and the false prophet must also be seen as fallen angels, that is, as demons only having male human appearance designed to deceive mankind on earth. What we need to grasp here is that when angelic beings – who are spirit beings, which do not have a body, nor are they visible – when these enter this physical world, they always take on male human appearance, which we see throughout God's word is indeed the case (noting for instance Luke 24:4,5 with Luke 24:22,23).

And that this evil trio here is the devil and two fallen angels as demons can be further grasped from what God tells us at Revelation 16:13,14, "[13] And I saw coming out of the mouth of the dragon and out of the mouth of the beast and out of the mouth of the false prophet, three unclean spirits like frogs; [14] for they are spirits of demons, performing signs, which go out to the kings of the whole world, to gather them together for the war of the great day of God, the Almighty."

What is critical for us to grasp here then is that what Satan, the devil, is attempting to do, in having the antichrist and the false prophet on the earth during this seven-year period, is to COUNTERFEIT GOD THE FATHER, THE SON OF GOD, AND THE HOLY SPIRIT! What this means then is that just as God The Father is always unseen, so the devil is unseen; and just as God The Father always works and speaks through His Son, The Lord Jesus Christ, Who is always the visible expression of God; then so too with the devil here, he works and speaks through the antichrist – who is called "antichrist," not only because he is opposed to Christ, but also because he attempts to counterfeit Christ, which is why, for instance, we see the antichrist pictured as having suffered a fatal blow and returned to life again at Revelation 13:3,12,14, simply because God's Son died and rose again from the dead again! So now the antichrist attempts to deceive mankind by doing the same, which is possible because angelic beings do not die, with only the human body they have ever dying. And then we are to see that just as The Holy Spirit is on the scene of earth to make God's Son known, so too do we see the false prophet do the same from the time he arises during the last three and a half years of the second age of time, in terms of focusing on the antichrist and seeking to make him known on earth!

So what we are to ever keep in mind as believers on earth at the present time is that what we have just been looking at from 2 Thessalonians 2:1-12 and Revelation 13:1-18, relating to the rule of antichrist as the political leader of a one world government and the false prophet as the leader of a one world false religious system, is that this is Satan's agenda, to establish this evil trio as ruling over the present earth, instead of God! Only believers on earth at present, as indwelt of The Holy Spirit, restrains and prevents Satan from carrying out his agenda; but that will end with our removal from the earth as God makes clear from 1 Thessalonians 4:14-17, which is an event under God's full control!

*At least ten things that Satan needs to have in place in order to bring his agenda to pass on earth*

And before we go on to the next chapter, we should further note that in order for Satan to bring his agenda to pass on earth, as we just saw at 2 Thessalonians 2 and Revelation 13, he obviously needs a number of things to be in place on earth as a minimum, which are as listed below and not limited to only this. What also needs to be grasped here is that ALL these things are being implemented at the same time and – as anyone knows who had been following these developments – they are being implemented at an exponential rate!

1) A one world government under one world political leader

2) A one world religion under one world religious leader

3) A cashless society, which requires the introduction of a digital currency

4) A digital identification mark (ID) as a means to control as to who buys and sells. This ID will be biometric in nature, that is, will use some part of the human body to identify that it is really you, such as one's face, a fingerprint, the iris of the eyes, or one's voice

5) Control of the media, so as to control what people hear, see, read, and therefore think

6) A surveillance state, so as to be able to not only identify individuals, but to also know where they are at any given time of the day or night, including knowing what they are doing

7) Control of the population, which includes population increases, by whatever means may be necessary to achieve this, such as mind control, drugs, eugenics, transhumanism, and so forth

8) A disarmed population, so that people cannot defend themselves, nor rise up against the established authorities

9) Killer robots, drones, and similar means to eliminate those who are deemed enemies of the state

10) Removal of the United States from being world leader economically, militarily, and diplomatically

In Chapter Six of Section 2, we will be giving links to videos and articles to show how the C-virus pandemic has been used by those perpetrating this viral outbreak so as to move us closer to the implementation of the above. Then, in Section 3 we will be looking at why President Trump and his administration; Q and the Q movement, believers worldwide; and God, are hated by Satan and the Deep State, and therefore, are seen as obstacles to be removed!

"the one who practices sin is of the devil, for the devil has sinned from the beginning. The Son of God appeared for this purpose, to destroy the works of the devil."

1 John 3:8

# CHAPTER FOUR

## The Deep State, as Satan's useful tool

Now that we have looked at the rise of Satan, the devil, and of his evil intentions, we are now in a better position to understand what the Deep State is. And what we are to understand at the outset is that Satan, as a fallen angelic being, operates from the spiritual world, which further means he does not have a body, so that he uses the Deep State, that is, human beings and human organizations on earth as a vehicle to work through, in order to accomplish his agenda!

So, the obvious question is: What is the deep state in practical terms? An answer would be that the Deep State can be regarded as the visible and invisible means of this earthly realm that Satan, the devil, uses since the time of Adam and Eve to accomplish his plans, during the four ages of time; which has the principal objective of replacing God with himself as god and with the intent of setting up his own world kingdom that would encompass the whole of creation for both time and eternity!

Those human beings and organizations that can be regarded as part of the Deep State all have one thing in common – whether they operate on a worldwide basis or just within one country – which is that they are all GLOBALISTS! And a globalist, or a globalist organization, all have the one goal, which is to work toward the establishment of a one world government for the solving of the problems of the human race on this earth!

And so, globalists believe that in order for a one world government to be established all countries need to set aside their sovereignty, while adopting open borders with unrestricted immigrant flow. This stands

*The Universal Postal Union (UPU)*

The Universal Postal Union is the primary forum for cooperation between postal sector players, helping to ensure a truly universal network of up-to-date products and services.

*The World Intellectual Property Organization (WIPO)*

The World Intellectual Property Organization protects intellectual property throughout the world through 23 international treaties.

*The World Meteorological Organization (WMO)*

The World Meteorological Organization facilitates the free international exchange of meteorological data and information and the furtherance of its use in aviation, shipping, security, and agriculture, among other things.

*The United Nations Educational, Scientific and Cultural Organization (UNESCO)*

The United Nations Educational, Scientific and Cultural Organization focuses on everything from teacher training to helping improve education worldwide. Its stated purpose is to contribute to peace and security by promoting international collaboration through educational, scientific, and cultural reforms in order to increase universal respect for justice, the rule of law, and human rights along with fundamental freedom proclaimed in the United Nations Charter.

As can be seen from the above PARTIAL LIST, the United Nations operates on a global scale and in every area of human life! But before we leave our look at the United Nations as the foremost visible vehicle being presently used by the Deep State globalists to bring in a one world government, we need to point out a very far reaching recent development at the United Nations, which was the GLOBAL COMPACT for MIGRATION (GCM), which was adopted by the UN general assembly on December 19, 2018. And what many are not aware of is that this compact MAKES MIGRATION A HUMAN RIGHT!

And so, let us keep in mind as we continue that the United Nations is simply a tool of the Deep State toward the establishment of a one world government!

## 2) World Economic Forum (WEF)

Another world body that the Deep State uses to push its globalist agenda of bringing in a one world government, apart from the United Nations, is the World Economic Forum, based in Geneva, Switzerland, and founded in 1971. The Forum's mission is to improve the state of the world by engaging business, political, academic, and other leaders of society to shape global, regional, and industry agendas. The WEF hosts an annual meeting at the end of January in Davos, Switzerland, for the English-speaking world, where some 2,500 business leaders, international political leaders, economists, celebrities and journalists gather for up to four days to discuss the most pressing issues facing the world.

The WEF further holds other non-English annual meetings, that being in China, India, and the United Arab Emirates, plus some six to eight regional meetings each year in locations across Africa, East Asia and Latin America. It also produces a series of research reports and engages its members in sector-specific initiatives. As is quite evident, the WEF seeks to especially provide a platform for leaders from all stakeholder groups from around the world – business, government and civil society – to come together.

## 3) Council on Foreign Relations (CFR)

Another influential Deep State instrument is the Council on Foreign Relations, which was founded in 1921 and is headquartered in New York City. It is a United States nonprofit think tank specializing in U.S. foreign policy and international affairs. Its membership, which numbers about 4,900, has included senior politicians, more than a dozen secretaries of state, CIA directors, bankers, lawyers, professors, and senior media figures.

The CFR meetings convene government officials, global business leaders and prominent members of the intelligence and foreign-policy community to discuss international issues. CFR publishes the bi-monthly journal Foreign Affairs, and runs the David Rockefeller Studies Program, which influences foreign policy by making recommendations to the presidential administration and diplomatic community, testifying before Congress, interacting with the media, and publishing on foreign policy issues.

*4) The Trilateral Commission*

Yet another influential Deep State instrument is the Trilateral Commission, which is a non-governmental, policy-oriented forum that was formed in 1973 by private citizens of Japan, North American nations (the U.S. and Canada), and Western European nations to foster substantive political and economic dialogue across the world. It brings together leaders in their individual capacity from the worlds of business, government, academia, press and media, as well as civil society. The Commission offers a global platform for open dialogue, reaching out to those with different views and engaging with decision makers from around the world with the aim of finding solutions to the great geopolitical, economic and social challenges of our time.

Its members are also committed to supporting a rules-based international system, closer cooperation across borders and respect for the diversity of approaches to policy issues. Here is a quote from its founding document, "Growing interdependence is a fact of life of the contemporary world. It transcends and influences national systems... While it is important to develop greater cooperation among all the countries of the world, Japan, Western Europe, and North America, in view of their great weight in the world economy and their massive relations with one another, bear a special responsibility for developing effective cooperation, both in their own interests and in those of the rest of the world."

*5) European Union (EU)*

Coming now to across the pond, we have the devil's second most important vehicle, after the United Nations, for forming a one world government, which is the European Union, which is a political and economic union of 28 member states that cover much of present-day Europe. It has a population of about 513 million and is the largest trading block in the world by GDP.

The EU has developed an internal single market through a standardized system of laws that apply in all member states, which have agreed to act as one. EU policies aim to ensure the free movement of people, goods, services and capital within the European Union. A monetary union was established in 1999 and 19 nations of the European Union currently use the euro currency. What is important to keep in mind here is that according to God's word the antichrist will arise from one of the countries of present-day Europe!

*6) Mainstream media*

Since globalists know that it is impossible to have a one world government without also controlling what people read, see, or hear, then they have made sure that they are in control of the mainstream media, which consists of every form of media that might be out there by which people receive the news, pertaining to what is going on in the world. Therefore, the mainstream media is to be seen as an integral and necessary part of the Deep State, for these people know that if they control the narrative, then they control the views that people hold regarding people and events occurring worldwide, even if that information is knowingly false. However, one thing is sure, the Deep State will make ensure that the narrative put forth is in line with the ideology that they want people to hold!

There are three short videos that would be very instructive to watch at this point. Since the first is titled, "QAnon: Killing the mocking bird media," then before watching this revealing video there are some terms which need to be understood, which are mentioned in the title and referenced in the video. The first is Q, which refers to the Q posts and subsequent movement that arose, which is the worldwide, that grew since October 28, 2017, when President Trump started communicating with his supporters by means of Q posts. And QAnons are simply researchers and decoders, who do the research and interpret the posts for those of the Q movement, since the Q posts themselves are often cryptic, being put out by military intelligence personnel working with President Trump and some of his staff at the White House. This will all be described in much greater detail in Chapter Nine, when we look at Q and the Q movement proper.

Then the term "mocking bird" is a secret program that the CIA developed in the 1950's to combat Communism, but which in our day is still ongoing and has now be weaponized to serve as a useful tool of the Deep State. Here is an excerpt from the information provided on the Q board, "Operation Mockingbird is a secret campaign by the US Central Intelligence Agency (CIA) to influence the media. The campaign recruits leading journalists into a network (Apache Group / SecureDrop) to control the daily news cycle and align the narrative to

CIA objectives. POTUS frequently attacks the Mainstream Media (MSM) because they are dishonest, corrupt, and the enemy of the American people. CIA uses the MSM as a PSYOP to brainwash the American people; non MSM platforms are cast as conspiracy and/or non-credible. MSM is fake news -- not to be trusted." Now that we have this as background, here is that very important short video,

https://www.youtube.com/watch?v=AHS0UjpM9sE.

A second short video, which will serve to reinforce what has just been said in the previous one is titled, "Proof that the news is scripted:"

https://www.youtube.com/watch?time_continue=93&v=eZVv2AOCnaA&feature=emb_logo .

Then a third very good short video is a Ted talk by Sharyl Attkisson, who is an investigative reporter. Her talk is titled, "Astroturf and the manipulation of media messages:"

https://www.youtube.com/watch?v=-bYAQ-ZZtEU.

## 7) Big Pharma

The term "Big Pharma" is being used here to identify an industry that developed in the United States in the early 1900's and has since spread worldwide, which has five main components that enables it to survive, these being the pharmaceutical companies, the doctors, the hospitals, the regulatory apparatus, and medical publications. And what is key to understanding Big Pharma is knowing that this industry is FOR PROFIT, which are derived from PATENTS of drugs or compounds that are MAN-MADE, that is, made in a laboratory.

What existed in the United States in the early 1900's was a system of health that had been a continuation of what had been practiced in Europe, especially, over the previous centuries, where the individual was treated by mostly natural means, with the underlying belief being that the body could heal itself if given the right conditions. This natural approach looked at the whole person, and especially one's diet, when seeking to help a person heal.

However, since anything that is found in nature cannot be patented, meant that one could not make any money off this system. And so in the early 1900's, the Carnegie Foundation commissioned a man named Abraham Flexner to visit all 155 medical schools then existing in the United States and Canada, resulting in the Flexner Report in 1910, which advocated for a medical system based on science, rather than what was then existing, with the model being advocated being that already in place at John Hopkins University School of Medicine in Baltimore, Maryland.

With this as background, one should now watch the following two videos, which have been carefully selected. The first one is titled, "Who made MD's king." It is a talk by a Naturopathic doctor and is very informative and revealing. And before one looks at the video, please be aware that this is part of a sales pitch for a network selling a brand of supplements. So, what I recommend here is just the first 45 minutes or so, where he shares the most valuable information that we should all be aware of regarding Big Pharma. So here is the video link,

https://www.youtube.com/watch?v=blxeEHV1lio

Then the second very informative and revealing video, which may make one cry, especially if one has lost loved ones to cancer, is titled, "Cancer: The Forbidden Cures," and will give one a good idea of the two system's approach to health now in place, which today are dubbed by the medical establishment as 'modern medicine' and 'alternative medicine:'

https://www.youtube.com/watch?v=zmQZcj3CggI

## 8) Word Government Summit

The World Government Summit is an annual event that has been held in Dubai, United Arab Emirates (UAE) since 2013, and now has about 150 countries participating. It is the only global organization dedicated to shaping the future of governments and setting the agenda for the next generation of governments worldwide. The World Government Summit brings together leaders in government for a global dialogue about governmental process and policies with a focus on the issues of futurism, technology and innovation. The summit acts as a knowledge exchange hub between government officials, thought leaders, policy makers and private sector leaders.

## 9) Singularity University (SU)

Another recent development, along with the World Government Summit, is Singularity University, which is actually a corporation established in Silicon Valley, California, in 2009, that also has the goal of preparing global leaders and institutions for the future. Its mission is to empower individuals and organizations across the globe to learn, connect, and innovate breakthrough solutions using accelerating technologies like artificial intelligence, robotics, and digital biology. To achieve this, they offer educational programs, courses, and summits; enterprise strategy, leadership, and innovation programs. The Singularity University community includes entrepreneurs, corporations, global nonprofits, governments, and academic institutions in more than 127 countries.

## 10) World Council of Churches (WCC)

Then there is the World Council of Churches, which is a worldwide inter-church organization founded in 1948 and based at the Ecumenical Centre in Geneva, Switzerland. The WCC is a worldwide fellowship of 349 global, regional and sub-regional, national and local church groups, seeking unity, a common witness and Christian service. The organization's members include denominations which claim to collectively represent some 590 million people across the world in about 150 countries, including 520,000 local congregations served by 493,000 pastors and priests, elders, teachers, members of parish councils and others. And although the Catholic Church is not a member, it still sends accredited observers to meetings.

What is important to observe here is that in the previous chapter, when looking at Revelation 13, as when the antichrist will be on earth as political leader of a one world government over the nations of the earth, he will have as assistant the false prophet, who is the religious leader of the false religious system of the earth, which we there saw had been instituted by Satan, the devil, back at the time of Cain.

And so, it is no coincidence to now see from this section that the globalist Deep State is seeking to move the nations of the world toward a unified mankind, along both political and religious lines, so that this world will then be ready for the introduction of the antichrist and the false prophet!

## B) Deep State world bodies operating secretly on earth

Now that we have looked at some of the VISIBLE human institutions of the Deep State that the devil uses in order to bring in a one world government, let us go on to look in this section at those human institutions, which although known by some, yet remain SECRETIVE as to the true nature of their operations. We will only deal with more current secret organizations here, which mean that there are many more, which date back centuries and these are still very much affecting our present world. And so, some of these secret institutions, organizations, or societies are:

### 1) Bilderberg Meeting

The Bilderberg Meeting, also unofficially called the "Bilderberg Group", "Bilderberg conference" or "Bilderberg Club," is an annual conference established in 1954 by Prince Bernhard of the Netherlands, which has the principal aim of fostering dialogue between Europe and North America. Participants are European and North American political leaders, experts from industry, finance, academia, and the media. The meetings are held under the Chatham House Rule, which states, "participants are free to use the information received, but neither the identity nor the affiliation of the speaker(s) nor of any other participant may be revealed," which is the main reason for it usually being designated as a secret society.

### 2) Freemasonry

Freemasonry is a secret fraternal (men-only) order of Free and Accepted Masons, the largest worldwide secret society. Spread by the advance of the British Empire, Freemasonry remains most popular in the British Isles and in other countries originally within the empire. Estimates of the worldwide membership of Freemasonry in the early 21st century ranged from about two million to more than six million.

Freemasonry evolved from the guilds of stonemasons and cathedral builders of the Middle Ages. With the decline of cathedral building, some lodges of masons began to accept honorary members to bolster their declining membership. From a few of these lodges developed modern symbolic or speculative Freemasonry, which particularly in the 17th and 18th centuries adopted the rites and trappings of ancient religious orders and of chivalric brotherhoods.

In addition to the main bodies of Freemasonry derived from the British tradition, there are also a number of appendant groups that are primarily social or recreational in character, having no official standing in Freemasonry but drawing their membership from the higher degrees of the society. They are especially prevalent in the United States and are among those known for their charitable work, such as the Ancient Arabic Order of the Nobles of the Mystic Shrine (the "Shriners"). In Britain and certain other countries there are separate lodges restricted to women.

*3) Bohemian Grove*

Bohemian Grove is an all-male secret society that is part of the Bohemian Club, which sits on a 2700-acre property in Monte Rio, California. It has been in operation since 1872 and is particularly famous due to its more than two-week July encampment of men of power, like former President Reagan, Clinton, Herbert H Bush and George W Bush, including many prominent business leaders, government officials, and senior media executives. Because of the high positions of the attendees, the property is equipped with year-round sophisticated security, including armed guards.

The main event of the summer gathering is 'The Cremation of Care' ceremony, which is a theatrical production in which some of the club's members participate as actors. The Cremation of Care was separated from the other Grove Plays in 1913 and moved to the first night and is said to have become "an exorcising of the demon to ensure the success of the ensuing two weeks." The ceremony takes place in front of the Owl Shrine. The moss and lichen-covered statue simulates a natural rock formation, yet holds electrical and audio equipment within it. One can get a good glimpse of the Bohemian Grove gathering and what goes on there from the video: https://www.youtube.com/watch?v=5UM3KbmfoG4

*4) Skull and Bones*

This secret society, founded in 1832 at Yale University in New Haven, Connecticut, is included here only because its members, who are all alumni of Yale, hold important positions in world affairs. For instance, Herbert H Bush, the 41st President of the United States, was a member before he died; as also his son, George W Bush, the 43rd President; and also John Kerry, former Presidential nominee for the Democratic Party and former Secretary of State under President Obama. Members, often referred to as 'Bonesmen,' meet in a building called 'the Tomb,' and also have a retreat on the St-Lawrence River called 'Deer Island.'

What would be useful at this point is give a link to a video presentation by Alex Newman, Foreign Correspondent for the New American magazine, which is a publication of the John Birch Society, which is an organization founded in 1958 by the Bible-believing Christian, Robert W Welch Jr, which has chapters nationwide. Here is the link to the video, which is titled, 'America under siege, the Deep State:' https://www.youtube.com/watch?v=6YUcUoFveJc. The value of this video is that it touches on some of the Deep State secret societies that we have just mentioned above.

*C) Puppet Masters exercising power and control over the Deep State worldwide*

As we close this chapter on the Deep State as Satan's useful tools on earth, we would be leaving out a very important component if we did not mention the puppet masters, who are and have been exercising power and control over the Deep State worldwide. These puppet masters consist of: 1) the House of Saud in Saudi Arabia; 2) the Rothschild families in Europe; and 3) George Soros in the United States. These three entities are exercising power and control worldwide and at every level due to their immense wealth, which is publicly unknown as to the exact amount, but is known to be in TRILLIONS of dollars multiple times over!

What needs to grasped here is that on the surface, these puppet masters earn their wealth by legitimate means. For instance, the House of Saud in Saudi Arabia made their fortune through owning a vast amount of oil; the Rothschilds through banking, as they own and control the central banks of every country on earth, except five; and George Soros' wealth is mostly through investments. However, a large part of their wealth is earned behind the scenes, through illegal activities, such as controlling the drug trade cartels and human trafficking rings worldwide!

We also need to be aware that they maintain their power and control through bribery of government officials, politicians, judges, lawyers, police officers, and so on, with no qualms in eliminating through death any person who dares to stand in their way! These people truly are the devil's principal tools operating as part of the Deep State on earth! We will have more to say on these puppet masters when we come to Chapter Nine and discuss Q and the Q movement.

## SECTION TWO

## SEEING THE C-VIRUS PANDEMIC AS THE OUTWORKING OF SATAN'S AGENDA BY MEANS OF THE DEEP STATE

# CHAPTER FIVE

## Five reasons why the C-virus outbreak should never have been called a pandemic!

What we will do in this second section of the book is to first give five reasons, here in Chapter Five, why the C-virus outbreak should never have been called a pandemic in the first place! Then we will go on in Chapter Six and show how this so-called pandemic has only served to further Satan's agenda of bringing in a new world order to prepare the way for the coming of the antichrist and the false prophet to this earth, doing so through the Deep State. And then in Chapter Seven, we will look at how Satan has used this so-called pandemic to greatly weaken, and especially try to eliminate, the foundations that God established for stable societies that stands in his way of bringing in a one world government through the Deep State!

So, let us be clear at the outset here, as we begin this chapter, that this C-VIRUS outbreak was a PLANNED EVENT BY THE DEEP STATE, AS SPURRED ON BY SATAN, TO PREPARE THE WORLD FOR THE COMING OF A ONE WORLD GOVERNMENT! We are not saying here that this virus was not real, for it was; nor that it was not serious, for it did kill a lot of people worldwide. However, the important fact to grasp is that by all accounts (outside the Deep State media narrative) this viral outbreak was man-made and planned to its minutest details before it even started, as we will see as we proceed!

Before we go to the five reasons, please listen to this medical doctor on twitter, which is very revealing to our discussion!

https://twitter.com/Kingfreespeech/status/1258628590926729217

*1) The C-virus has been shown to be far less serious and lethal than the seasonal flu, so why lockdown one's economy?*

So the first reason why the C-virus outbreak should never have been called a pandemic by the director of the World Health Organization (WHO) on March 11, 2020, is that it has been conclusively shown to be far less serious and lethal than the seasonal flu, which is not being called a pandemic; nor does it result in whole countries being shut down, even though it annually kills far more people worldwide! And one word of caution here: Please do not take your information on this controversial matter from Google, as they are part of the Deep State, and they are most definitely censoring all but the narrative that they want you to hear, see, and believe regarding this event!

Therefore, one is left perplexed as to why this particular viral outbreak would close down economy after economy worldwide, when no pandemic from the past – with some being far more serious viral outbreaks – never having necessitated such a drastic measure! Therefore, the only conclusion that one can come to is that there has to be some sinister forces at work here!

Below are two articles that the reader will find very useful to this discussion. The first is titled, "Coronavirus deaths by age: How it's like (and not like) other disease:"

https://www.bloomberg.com/opinion/articles/2020-05-07/comparing-coronavirus-deaths-by-age-with-flu-driving-fatalities

The second is titled, "The flu, the coronavirus, and hospital beds:"

https://www.americanthinker.com/articles/2020/04/the_flu_the_coronavirus_and_hospital_beds.html

*2) The C-virus has been shown, in all countries alike, to kill mostly the elderly*

A second important reason why this viral outbreak should never have been called a pandemic is due to the fact that in all countries where the C-virus occurred, more than 80 percent of deaths were of people over 65 years old! And since, as we have seen above, this virus is far less serious than the seasonal flu, then why close down schools, or any place of business for that matter, since nothing is ever shut down for the yearly flu, which also kills mostly the elderly?

Again, since this defies logic, then the only conclusion that one can come up with here is that there are sinister forces at work! Below are two articles that are very helpful to the discussion. The first is especially since it has a lot of links to other articles that also has valuable information. It is titled, "Coronavirus hype is the greatest political hoax in history:"

https://www.washingtontimes.com/news/2020/apr/28/coronavirus-hype-biggest-political-hoax-in-history/

The second article, which is very relevant, is titled, "Why are older people more at risk of coronavirus?:"

https://theconversation.com/why-are-older-people-more-at-risk-of-coronavirus-133770

*3) In almost all the cases of C-virus infection resulting in death, those who died had one or more medical preconditions*

A third very good reason for why this viral infection should never have been called a pandemic is that almost all those who were infected with the virus and subsequently died, were persons with one or more medical preconditions, such as diabetes, high blood pressure, a weakened heart, or other ailment, which meant they had a compromised immune system to begin with! Almost all persons getting infected with the virus, who did not have a medical precondition and had a well-functioning immune system, recovered within a relatively short period of time, with few ever requiring hospitalization.

This then again begs the question: So why shut down a whole society for one segment that is already medically compromised, which leads again to only one answer, which is that there are sinister forces at work here! Below is a fact sheet from the Centers for Disease Control and Prevention (CDC), which was produced for health professionals. It is titled, "People who are at higher risk for severe illness:"

https://www.cdc.gov/coronavirus/2019-ncov/hcp/underlying-conditions.html

*4) Countries that did not lockdown and continued all activities as before the pandemic, did not incur any more cases of C-virus infection than those nations that did shut down*

A fourth very good reason why the C-virus outbreak should never have been called a pandemic is that in at least two countries, Sweden and Belarus, there was no shutdown of the country's businesses or schools, which meant that people came and went as before the pandemic, with no more cases of C-virus being recorded than countries that did shut down! They simply relied on the scientific fact of 'herd immunity,' which states that as more and more people come in contact with this virus, as with others like for the common cold and the seasonal flu, one's immune system will in the majority of cases build up antibodies.

Please note the following, which is titled, "Didier Raoult: Government study in Spain finds those who kept working were less infected than those in lockdown:"

https://www.thegatewaypundit.com/2020/05/didier-raoult-government-study-spain-finds-kept-working-less-infected-lockdown/

And here is a useful article titled, "Life has to go on: How Sweden has faced the virus without a lockdown:"

https://www.nytimes.com/2020/04/28/world/europe/sweden-coronavirus-herd-immunity.html

Three other countries, namely South Korea, Singapore, and Hong Kong, also had no lockdown of their countries, although strict measures were applied to those who had the virus. Below is a relevant article on this discussion, titled, "How South Korea reigned in the outbreak without shutting everything down:"

https://www.npr.org/sections/goatsandsoda/2020/03/26/821688981/how-south-korea-reigned-in-the-outbreak-without-shutting-everything-down

What this means then is that – as it has been widely reported outside the mainstream media – since this viral infection was not more serious than the seasonal flu, meant people needed to take precautions, but life could go on, and should have gone on, as normal! This further means that there should not have been drastic measures like the shutdown of whole countries. And the fact that this did happen again begs the question: Why did it happen?

*5) Since the C-virus was a planned event, then it should never have been called a pandemic, but rather should be called a hoax, since its only purpose was to further a sinister agenda*

Then a fifth reason why this viral outbreak should never have been called a pandemic is due to the fact that the C-virus pandemic was a planned event! That this was so can be gathered from the fact that the director of the World Health Organization (WHO) advised countries on January 9th, 2020, against the application of any trade or travel restrictions on China. The question is: Why would he say that when there was a lockdown imposed on the city of Wuhan on January 23, 2020, where the outbreak began sometime in mid-December or earlier, and around 5 million people had already left the city without being screened?

Since thousands of Companies from all parts of the world have set up shop in China over the last twenty years, it was only to be expected that many foreign nationals would be travelling to and from China, therefore easily spreading any viruses that originated in China to their own country! This would no doubt be a fact that the WHO would have known! So why advise against travel restrictions on China? Was the WHO and China in partnership to knowingly spread the coronavirus so as to cause a pandemic? Evidence coming out now certainly seems to indicate that! Please note the following report from Israel's national news network alleging exactly that:

https://www.israelnationalnews.com/News/News.aspx/279992

What is also incomprehensible – and is another reason why there has to be a dark agenda in play here – is that on January 30th, 2020, the director of the WHO actually referred to the outbreak as a global health emergency – which is not a pandemic – and again strongly opposed any travel or trade restrictions against China, or any other measures! The additional question here is: If this is a global emergency and the source of the outbreak is known to be Wuhan, China, which is already under lockdown, then would it not be prudent to restrict travel and trade from that area of China at the very least?

Even as late as February 29th, 2020, the director of the WHO was advising against the imposition of trade or travel restrictions of any country experiencing outbreaks! Again, the question is: Why? And one will continue to ask such questions until one comes to realize that the director of WHO, Tedros Adhanom Ghebreyesus, was actually selected for the post by Bill Gates! And what one should know about Bill Gates here is that he is the third largest donor to the WHO, through his Bill and Melinda Gates Foundation, after the United States and China! And what is really revealing is that Bill Gates was already calling the C-virus outbreak a pandemic on February 28, 2020, about twelve days BEFORE it was announced as such by the director of the WHO on March 11th, 2020! Please note the following article by Bill Gates, where this viral outbreak is called a pandemic in his first paragraph:

https://www.gatesnotes.com/Health/How-to-respond-to-COVID-19?WT.mc_id=20200228175011_COVID19_BG-TW&WT.tsrc=BGTW&linkId=83234892

So, did Bill Gates know something that the rest of us did not? The answer to that question might be partly answered in the fact that this C-virus pandemic was actually SIMULATED DOWN TO ITS MINUTEST DETAILS back on October 18, 2019, at Event 201, which was a simulation of a coronavirus outbreak, which turned into a pandemic. This simulation was sponsored by the Bill and Melinda Gates Foundation, the Rockefeller Institute, and the World Economic Forum – all globalist entities – and was held at John Hopkin's Center for Health Security in New York. Please watch the video below of this event and you will see how carefully planned this event was, especially how it was determined in advance how competing views with the official narrative were going to be handled. The title of the video is: "Did Bill Gates & World Economic Forum Predict the Coronavirus Outbreak?:"

https://www.bitchute.com/video/4ZCrjFTh86JC/

What is even scarier to contemplate is that Bill Gates already has plans for C-virus PHASE TWO! One wishes this was a joke, but unfortunately it is not. Please watch the video below, which is titled, "Fear is a Weapon: Bill Gates, Phase Two is a Bioterror attack:"

https://www.youtube.com/watch?v=BYPPY4IXgSA

A lot of Bill Gates motives for his actions and statements will come to light in the next chapter, where we post further videos on his activities.

And so, we are to see that there are definite sinister forces at work to bring a certain agenda to pass, which involves some very wealthy individuals, such as Bill Gates and George Soros; and organizations such as the United Nations; political parties, such as the Democrats in the US; and also countries, such as China, which certainly appear to be colluding together with a host of other individuals, organizations, and countries to bring in an agenda as part of this C-virus pandemic! This should already be clear from some of the articles and videos already provided as part of this book, and will be further confirmed as we continue in the next chapter and also in the third section of the book.

At the start of this chapter, the following statement was made, "So, let us be clear at the outset here, as we begin this chapter, that this C-virus outbreak was a PLANNED EVENT BY THE DEEP STATE, AS SPURRED ON BY SATAN, TO PREPARE THE WORLD FOR THE COMING OF A ONE WORLD GOVERNMENT " If you are still not convinced of that as we close this chapter, then please watch the following two very explosive videos! The first is significantly titled, "Plandemic Documentary: The hidden agenda:"

https://www.bitchute.com/video/IB3ijQuLkkUr/

The second is titled, "Dr Andrew Kaufman: They want to genetically modify us:"

https://www.altcensored.com/

"Woe to those who call evil good, and good evil; Who substitute darkness for light and light for darkness…"

Isaiah 5:20 in part


"Do not participate in the unfruitful works of darkness, but instead even expose them…"

Ephesians 5:11

# CHAPTER SIX

## How Satan has furthered his agenda through the C-virus pandemic, as assisted by the Deep State

What would now be important to consider in this chapter is how Satan has used this so-called pandemic to further his agenda, as assisted by the Deep State. And here we will use the list of ten items that we earlier identified at the end of Chapter Three to guide us, as things that are necessary for Satan to accomplish in order to bring in the antichrist and the false prophet to this earth, as part of his new world order. Again, let us keep in mind that ALL these things are being implemented AT THE SAME TIME, and at exponential speed! So what follows are carefully selected articles and videos with that itemized list in mind, as things being furthered through the C-virus pandemic. For maximum effect, please watch all the videos and read all of the articles. And please remember that some of the videos provide information on more than one item on the list.

*1) A one world government under one world political leader*

Video title, "Henry Kissinger & Bill Gates call for mass vaccination & global governance:"

https://www.bitchute.com/video/myqVcFYIc0An/

*2) A one world religion under one world religious leader*

The following two videos are by a believer who was formerly a medic in the Coast Guard. The first video is titled, "All they wanna do is crown their beast king:"

https://www.youtube.com/watch?v=uER1Tj32L04

The second video is titled, "It was always about the aftermath and not the event." It is recommended that only the first 55 minutes of this video be watched, as there are a few words of coarse language in two of the clips being shown in the second half.

https://www.youtube.com/watch?v=RX2mSAiZiwg

3) *A cashless society, which requires the introduction of a digital currency*

Video title, "Coronavirus endgame: The economic crisis & rollout of the new digital financial system:"

https://www.bitchute.com/video/weHhvw2W4vNH/

Video title, "China's great leap to wallet-free living:"

https://www.youtube.com/watch?v=75AXINUL47g

4) *A digital identification mark (ID) as a means to control who buys and sells. This ID will be biometric in nature, that is, will use some part of the human body to identify that it is really you, such as one's face, a fingerprint, the iris of the eyes, one's voice, or some implanted device like a chip*

Video title, "A.I Supremacy 2020 | Rise of the Machines - "Super" Intelligence Quantum Computers:"

https://www.youtube.com/watch?v=nvPDEK776qo

Video title, "ID2020 + central banking digital currency = NOW

https://www.youtube.com/watch?v=euJoZLcPKf4

5) *Control of the media, so as to control what people hear, see, read, and think*

Video title, "Cop fired for posting this anti-lockdown rant!:"

https://www.youtube.com/watch?time_continue=82&v=hbKkfNS_SIA&feature=emb_logo

The following article link is useful for its example of the level of "groupthink" that tech companies want to achieve by censoring conservative voices in societies worldwide, which is very much as

George Orwell described in his novel "1984." This link concerns a video that Michelle Malkin posted on Tweeter regarding big tech censorship, which President Trump retweeted, and which Tweeter then deleted! Watch:

https://www.thegatewaypundit.com/2020/05/wow-president-trump-retweets-michelle-malkin-video-big-tech-censorship-twitter-censors-tweet-deletes-video/

*6) A surveillance state, so as to be able to not only identify individuals, but to also know where they are at any time of the day or night, including knowing what they are doing*

Video Title, "You're being watched right now:"

https://www.youtube.com/watch?v=c8jDsg-M6qM

Video title, "Rockefeller blue print for pandemic police state exposed:"

https://www.bitchute.com/video/N9KNZknx7Fer/

*7) Control of the population by whatever means may be necessary to achieve this, such as mind control, vaccines, drugs, eugenics, transhumanism, and so forth*

Video title, "It is not about a virus, but about control!:"

https://www.youtube.com/watch?v=DgQNmMih-vc

Video title, "Elon Musk's plan to merge humans with A.I.:"

https://www.youtube.com/watch?v=4fGYT-gIICA

The following video was another one that YouTube censored regarding the current pandemic. The video title is, "Dr Tenpenny: This is the biggest scam ever perpetrated on the human race:"

https://www.bitchute.com/video/DaJYIaCdDfQ4/

Video title, "Bill Gates: Test tube meat, mandatory vaccinations & real time global surveillance from space:"

https://www.youtube.com/watch?v=eRRxreQxIV8

*8) A disarmed population, so that people cannot defend themselves, nor rise up against the established authorities*

The following article, which is titled, "Police state dry run a huge success," has many, many links to other articles and sources of useful information:

https://www.americanthinker.com/articles/2020/05/police_state_dry_run_a_huge_success.html

Article title, "PM Trudeau begins the process of disarming Canadians:"

https://www.americanthinker.com/blog/2020/05/pm_trudeau_begins_the_process_of_disarming_canadians.html

*9) Killer robots, drones, and other means to eliminate those who are deemed enemies of the state*

The next two amazing videos should be of concern to all of us! The first video is titled, "A.I. is making it easier to kill (you):"

https://www.youtube.com/watch?v=GFD_Cgr2zho

The second video shows how the robots have been programmed to kill only certain individuals. Video title, "New robot makes solders obsolete:"

https://www.youtube.com/watch?v=y3RIHnK0_NE

*10) Removal of the United States from being world leader economically, militarily, and diplomatically*

One obvious way to remove the United States from its position as world leader is to deal with the President, especially when that President is a nationalist and is totally against a globalist agenda, as is clear from one of President Trump's latest addresses to the United Nations:

https://news.un.org/en/story/2018/09/1020472

This then brings up three relevant questions relating to the present subject and the C-virus pandemic:

1) The first question is: If this is about the virus, and not the 2020 Presidential election, then why are Democratic states, like California, keeping their state closed, while inflating C-virus death numbers, and at the same time sending all voters mail-in ballots for an election that is six months away, and doing this by executive order of the governor, Gavin Newsom?

Article title, "San Diego County supervisor says six of 194 confirmed deaths are 'pure, solely coronavirus' deaths:"

https://www.washingtonexaminer.com/news/san-diego-county-supervisor-says-six-of-194-confirmed-deaths-are-pure-solely-coronavirus-deaths

Article title, "Newsom signs executive order declaring California a vote-by-mail state:"

https://www.cbsnews.com/news/newsom-signs-executive-order-declaring-california-a-vote-by-mail-state-2020-05-08/

2) The second question is: If this is about the virus and not the 2020 Presidential election, then why is it that the states that have Democratic governors are showing the largest number of cases and deaths of C-virus, as compared to states having Republican governors?

Article title, "Virus deaths in Democratic versus Republican states:"

https://lawliberty.org/virus-deaths-in-democratic-versus-republican-states/

3) And then the third question is: If this is about the virus and not the 2020 Presidential election, then why is Big Pharma against the use of a known and existing cure, such as hydroxychloroquine, which President Trump introduced earlier on as a possible game-changer?

Title of this article, "Is Big Pharma behind the great war on hydroxychloroquine?:"

https://www.americanthinker.com/blog/2020/05/is_big_pharma_behind_the_great_war_on_hydroxychloroquine.html

Article title, "Fauci knew about HCQ in 2005 – nobody needed to die:"

https://onenewsnow.com/perspectives/bryan-fischer/2020/04/27/fauci-knew-about-hcq-in-2005-nobody-needed-to-die

Video title, "Hydroxychloroquine:"

https://www.altcensored.com/watch?v=zB-_SV-y11Y

Is the only reason that Big Pharma is against the use of hydroxychloroquine because it is a natural compound, which means that it cannot be patented? Which further means that they cannot make any money off its use? Or is the reason because they want a vaccine cure instead, by which they can make billions? Or is the reason because as part of the Deep State they do not want a cure now, for this means an end to the C-virus pandemic and a return to work for workers, thereby destroying their plan to cripple the economy so that President Trump would not be re-elected in November 2020? Are all three of these reasons valid?

"If the foundations are destroyed, what can the righteous do?"

Psalm 11:3



"But realize this, that in the last days difficult times will come. For men will be lovers of self, lovers of money, boastful, arrogant, revilers, disobedient to parents, ungrateful, unholy, unloving, irreconcilable, malicious gossips, without self-control, brutal, haters of good, treacherous, reckless, conceited, lovers of pleasure rather than lovers of God, holding to a form of godliness, although they have denied its power; avoid such men as these."

2 Timothy 3:1-5

## CHAPTER SEVEN

## How Satan has used the C-virus pandemic and the Deep State to weaken and seek to eliminate the foundations that God established for stable societies

In this chapter, we will look at the HUMAN COST involved, which is a direct result of the coronavirus being called a pandemic by the WHO. And by 'human cost' we mean the untold suffering that has been experienced by families and individuals worldwide, which was definitely not an act of God, like a tornado or a hurricane, but was the direct result of evil forces behind the scenes working through useful tools on earth that has come to be called the Deep State!

On a personal level, that human cost was brought close to home recently when I was out doing my grocery shopping. As I drove into the parking lot of a local grocery store, there was a woman on the sidewalk out front with a large sign beside her, which read, "Will clean house for groceries." After parking the car, I went and talked with her and found out she was a widow, her husband having died seven years ago, and now she was left to raise their two sons, aged 12 and 13. She said that before this pandemic, she used to clean houses for a living. But now, with people either quarantined, working from home, or laid off, it meant that she had not been able to find enough work to pay all her expenses, being already in arrears on her utilities and no gas in her car.

She said that the three of them had porridge for breakfast that morning and were scheduled to have the same again for supper that evening. When I told her I would help her, she immediately exclaimed, "Praise be to Jesus!," which prompted me to inquire as to whether she was a Christian, to which she said 'yes.'

God tells us at 1 John 3:17,18, "But whoever has the world's goods, and sees his brother in need and closes his heart against him, how does the love of God abide in him? Little children, let us not love with word or with tongue, but in deed and truth." In other words, sometimes true help can only come by opening our wallets, something God was leading me to do here, whether this woman was a Christian or not. But since she was, then that was an even greater compelling reason to help her, since we were part of the same family of God.

And so, let us keep two very salient points in mind here, as we read the rest of this chapter. The first is that a lot of the measures enacted were due to one single fact, in that it was determined earlier on that this particular virus, which is of the same family as the seasonal flu, somehow needed SOCIAL DISTANCING of at least six feet! What this meant then is that this necessitated the closure of all activities of a public nature, where people could be expected to be in close proximity, such as work places, schools, places of worship, sporting events and so forth. But what if whoever came up with this hypothesis was wrong? Do we not first question one's hypothesis that will affect the livelihood of countless millions, even billions, worldwide before we adopt them? Below is a useful article on this subject, titled, "Social distancing is snake oil, not science:"

https://www.americanthinker.com/articles/2020/05/social_distancing_is_snake_oil_not_science.html

Then the second very important point to keep in mind is that those bearing the brunt of this man-made virus and needless pandemic were SENIORS, since not only do they form the largest group of those who died from this virus, but they are also the group that has suffered the most in terms of the human cost due to this virus having been called a pandemic. For what needs to be grasped here is that every seniors' home was closed even to families and caregivers, which meant that these seniors who died did so without their families being present, and even those that did not die, suffered greatly from not being able to see their families and friends, or partake in any activities, as most were curtailed. This then makes what is written here even more painful to digest!

Since this virus was active in China almost three months before it was declared a pandemic, would not China and the WHO have known that almost only seniors were at real risk? So, no wonder that President Trump has now cut off all funding to the WHO, which will have an impact and send a clear message since the United States is its largest donor at the tune of 443 million dollars a year!

And so, what we need to keep in mind as we continue is that the PANIC AND FEAR that has stirred populations worldwide into a FRENZY has caused people everywhere to become DISORIENTED, due to seeing the C-virus pandemic develop as it did on a worldwide scale, thereby causing many people to be left in a state of UNCERTAINTY as to what this all means and what happens next.

But let us be clear here that Satan had very specific goals in view in pushing this C-virus pandemic through the Deep State, which consists of the REMOVAL OF THE FOUNDATIONS that make for STABLE SOCIETIES! In other words, it is not in the devil's best interest, if he is to bring in his evil agenda to this world, to have all the INSTITUTIONS that God established remain in place, such as the FAMILY UNIT, which consists of a husband, wife, and children, or have PLACES OF WORSHIP of the One true God remain open, which strengthens people of faith through their gathering to hear the word of God and to support one another through meeting together as a local church family.

It is also not in Satan's best interest to have people gainfully employed at MEANINGFUL WORK to earn their living in order to support their families. It is also not in Satan's best interest to have the RULE OF LAW followed, where there is a moral code based on God's word in place to govern societies, so that they do not digress into barbaric states. Therefore, these are the foundations that the devil has sought to destroy, or at least greatly weaken, through this pandemic; for he knows that if these foundations be destroyed, then he will have total population control, which he needs in order for his agenda to succeed!

It has been well said that 'it is easier to build strong children than to repair broken men.' And there is no better way to have broken men than by destroying the family unit and by preventing men from being gainfully employed to provide for their families! Getting paid for what one did not earn only leads to a dependency that eventually destroys the individual and the society. So as we continue, let us see if these things are not at play in what we now consider.

*Businesses being closed worldwide, except for those deemed as essential services, therefore putting millions of people out of work*

Never in the history of the world, not even during the first or second world war, have we ever seen businesses being MANDATED TO CLOSE by national, state, or local governments, resulting in millions of people being thrown out of work and forced to rely on government handouts to pay bills, such as mortgages, rent, utilities, and food.

Business owners themselves, of those which were forced by law to close, face a dire situation, as most have rent, utilities, and other expenses relating to running a business, and yet no income to pay those expenses. They too were forced to rely on government loans and grants, where those were even available. However, the sad truth is that many will not be able to survive and will be closing their doors.

*Schools closed worldwide, not only at the elementary level, but also institutions of higher learning*

What is unprecedented was to see all schools closed, not just at the elementary level, but also at the college and university level. And what is just as bad is that many governments have now decided to leave these schools closed for the duration of this school year. What this has meant in many cases is parents, who are at home, are forced to teach their children, either through lessons being sent over the internet, or through some other means.

What is difficult to understand through all this is not only are the children being dumbed down through the current curriculum, but the jobs being required due to the large scale drive to near complete automation in all areas of life, from banking to trucking, and from the grocery store to the manufacturing plant, all require knowledge and skills that are now a necessity to maneuver through the robotics and artificial intelligence that many of these new jobs demand.

Below are three important videos that gives us an idea of the cutting edge technologies and the jobs required in each of these areas that are coming on stream, and please ask yourself as you watch whether this pandemic seemed to have made it easier for students to be

FORCED in the near future to depend on transhumanism, that is, the meshing of some part of the human body with artificial intelligence in order to accomplish these tasks? In other words, as we have seen in the last chapter, is not part of the plan here to force those coming into the workforce in the near future to somehow be meshed with artificial intelligence in order to carry out the tasks required to earn a living? Even with 21 years of formal education, including an Engineering degree, I have difficulty keeping up with all the new scientific advances behind all this technology, let alone having to apply it in a practical way in a job every day!

So the first relevant short video to watch here is titled, "15 biggest technology trends in 2020:"

https://www.youtube.com/watch?v=_kQsb1HeHtU

And the second video is titled, "Gartner top 10 strategic technology trends for 2020:"

https://www.youtube.com/watch?v=6HzdOkPPPRU

And the third eye-opening video is titled, "Artificial Intelligence Advancements That Are Going To Change The Future Forever:"

https://www.youtube.com/watch?v=DWHXZ38KQiM

*All sports, cultural activities, and even parks, and recreation areas being closed worldwide*

What was also beyond the incredulous was to see all sports come to a halt worldwide, and not just sports at all levels, but also the stoppage of all cultural activities and the closure of even parks and recreational areas! Even the Olympics, which were scheduled to be held in Tokyo in July 2020 were postponed until 2021.

What this means then is that there were no activities outside the home that were available for families to partake in, being effectively quarantined to one's home, whether one liked it or not. Even outdoor skate parks were closed, and in California they even bulldozed one full of sand to prevent the kids from using it! But ingenuity prevailed and some were back with dirt bikes the next day!

*Due to social distancing rules, even conferences, weddings, and funerals entered into totally new territory*

Imagine having a wedding already planned during the time the pandemic was in effect? Plans would have been made a long time ahead, and in some cases, invitations would have been sent out. With travel restrictions and social distancing rules in place, the airlines, buses, car rentals, hotels, restaurants, and motels were mostly all closed, which also made it impossible to hold conferences and meetings, which meant turning to other means instead, such as videoconferencing.

*Visiting restrictions on nursing homes, homes for the aged, and senior residences has been the biggest source of hardship, not only for seniors, but also for families, staff, and the seniors themselves*

Because the C-virus struck mostly seniors, then this meant that every facility in the world that housed seniors bore the brunt of the human suffering, for not only were many seniors dying (although the numbers were much lower than deaths from the seasonal flu), but because of the widespread disinformation regarding this virus, families and caregivers were restricted from access to those seniors in their hour of greatest need!

As one who is in his thirtieth year of working with seniors, and having also written a book on seniors ("So, I Hear You Want To Work With Seniors?"), I am painfully aware that most will decline cognitively even faster due to being shut in for any extended period of time. Even under the most ideal circumstances, that decline occurs the moment they become a resident! And since they know that this is not their home, what they look forward to the most are family visits from their children, grandchildren, and friends, which has been denied to them through this viral outbreak having been called a pandemic, when in reality there has never been a need for any of this to occur!.

And so, as we bring this chapter to a close, let us take all that has been said above and think about the human cost; about the needless emotional, physical, and mental suffering that has taken place and is still going on, which will no doubt leave scars for many years to come, depending on how long God allows this evil to persist. The following two articles and one video have been included here to help bring out the seriousness of the human cost involved due to this viral outbreak having been called a pandemic. The first article is titled, "Better safe than sorry?:"

https://www.americanthinker.com/blog/2020/05/better_safe_than_sorry.html

The second article is titled, "5 signs your coronavirus anxiety is threatening your mental health:"

https://www.newsmax.com/health/health-news/mental-health-anxiety-stress-lockdown/2020/05/05/id/966163/

The following video is being provided here because it will help to summarize a lot of what has been said in this second section, and in this chapter in particular. The title of the video is, "Dr. Ericson's briefing," which features a medical doctor in California, who with his associates, has done two months of research on this virus and then called in the media to present the findings. This news conference was so explosive that it has been banned on media platforms such as YouTube, Google, Facebook, Twitter, etc. In any case, here is the link, and believer me, this is worth the time spent to watch it:

https://www.bitchute.com/video/WaL7bJe5R1W2/

# SECTION THREE

# PRESIDENT TRUMP, Q, BELIEVERS, AND GOD ACTING TO RESTRAIN SATAN IN CARRYING OUT HIS AGENDA

"Put on the full armor of God, so that you will be able to stand firm against the schemes of the devil. For our struggle is not against flesh and blood, but against the rulers, against the powers, against the world forces of this darkness, against the spiritual forces of wickedness in the heavenly places."

Ephesians 6:11,12

# CHAPTER EIGHT

## President Trump and his administration

As was mentioned earlier in Chapter Four, President Trump is a nationalist, which means he is for sovereign nation states, also advocating for secure borders and a control on immigration flow into a country, which is the opposite of what globalists want, which well characterizes the Deep State. And of course, as long as President Trump is in office, then he is holding the line, from a physical standpoint, on Satan bringing in a one world government through the Deep State, which he needs in order to bring his agenda to pass.

What is also important to realize here is that the United States, of which President is effectively the CEO of, is the acknowledged leader of the world – economically, militarily, and diplomatically! What this means then, in practical terms, is that President Trump is the elephant in the room, which means that when he speaks and what he does has an immediate impact on the rest of the world, which nations readily acknowledge.

And what is crucial for us to grasp here in regards to our present subject is that President Trump did not seek the Presidency, but rather had been recruited by US military leaders, the large part of which had been purged from the military by President Obama due to not supporting his agenda. These military leaders also knew from the military intelligence that they had that Mr Trump was a capable candidate for restoring the United States to a path that would take it from its then downward slide into becoming a banana republic. These leaders also knew that Mr Trump had the knowledge and intelligence required for the task, plus, from their assessment – and this is important – did not have any skeletons in his closet!

Two very short videos have been selected to show what has just been stated. The first video is titled, "This will get Donald Trump elected," and was put out by his campaign just before the 2016 Presidential election, and it clearly shows 'why' Mr Trump was really running for President!

https://www.youtube.com/watch?v=G2qIXXafxCQ

The second video is titled "The second American Revolution is underway. Military Intelligence, QAnon, and President Trump." It was put out after President Trump had been elected and clearly lays out the reason for his election as President.

https://www.youtube.com/watch?v=j1rjiJgM8_g

Then what is also true is that 2020 is a Presidential election year, which means that if the Deep State – which in the United States takes in the Democratic party and the mainstream media – were able to remove him through impeachment, or defeat him at the ballot box, then on the human level at least that would mean that they would be able to retake control again and effectively stop President Trump and his administration from continuing to expose their deep corruption and outright treason during the years the Obama administration was in power, and which continued even after Mr Trump had been elected President! Then on the spiritual level, it would be paving the way for a one world government and so fall right in line with Satan's agenda of bringing in the antichrist and the false prophet.

And of course, we cannot forget China's complicity here. When this C-virus pandemic was called by the WHO, China had just signed the first phase of a trade agreement with the Trump administration, one that was definitely not in China's interest as a Communist regime, but which they had no choice in signing, for they knew that President Trump held all the leverage. In other words, China needs the US market to survive economically, but the US market does not need the Chinese market. The US only needs to bring back the manufacturing that Obama knowingly caused to move to China during his eight-year tenure, as part of his plan to weaken the United States economically and militarily in order to usher in a one world government.

What this means then is that China certainly had a lot to gain in unleashing this C-virus on the world, which they knew the WHO would then be calling a pandemic, and so the Deep State was aware that when this virus hit the United States, it would be devastating economically, which further meant that it would help the Democratic party gain the upper hand, if they could keep this pandemic going until election time on November 3, 2020; something that we have seen the Deep State do all they could to indeed cause this to happen, being vehemently opposed to any talk of re-opening the country again, as only one example!

One very telling sign that there was collusion between the Democratic party, the mainstream media, the WHO, Bill Gates, Big Pharma, and China here, in unleashing this pandemic on the world, and the United States in particular, can be seen from the moment that President Trump announced at one of his daily press briefing in late March that Hydroxychloroquine might be a game changer, which brought immediate and sustained opposition from the above mentioned Deep State entities!

For these Deep State entities very well knew that if this drug, in conjunction with two others – that have already been approved by the Food and Drug Administration (FDA) for other diseases and ailments, such as malaria, lupus, and arthritis – then that would mean that there was a known cure for the C-virus, therefore immediately bringing an end to this pandemic, and also to this Deep State's house of cards, including the need for a worldwide vaccine, as being pushed by Bill Gates, the WHO, and big Pharma! And so, it does not take rocket science to see that President Trump and his administration is a hindrance and very bid stumbling block to the Deep State's dream of one world government, which would be right in line with Satan's agenda!

Let us close this chapter with this quote from the White House:

'Quarantine' is when you restrict the movement of sick people. 'Tyranny' is when you restrict the movement of healthy people!

"For nothing is hidden that will not become evident, nor anything secret that will not be known and come to light."

Luke 8:17

# CHAPTER NINE

## Q and the Q movement

An obvious question that some might have here, who are not already familiar with Q, is: What is Q? In the previous chapter, we have stated that Donald John Trump was recruited for President by the US military leaders, who were in the know as to what Obama had been in the process of doing to the US, in terms of knowingly weakening the country both militarily and economically. So, after President Trump was elected on November 4, 2016, and then inaugurated formally into office on January 20, 2017, it then became crystal to all those working with him in his administration, by the time October rolled around, that the mainstream media was only going to put out fake news, or else skew the news is such a way as to cast President Trump in a negative light, so as to control the narrative that they wanted the American public to hear, see, and believe, thereby seeking to turn people against President Trump!

So on October 28, 2017, President Trump and a team consisting of military and civilian advisers started posting information on a private information board (4 Chan at first, then 8 Chan, and today 8 Kun), which is anonymous in nature, and which was signed in the bottom as simply 'Q.' This information, which was often cryptic in nature and often needed decoding to understand, nevertheless was such that it countered the lies and fake news of the mainstream media with the truth.

As word got around regarding this information, it quickly spread especially among President Trump's supporters, who came to realize through the Q posts that this – along with President Trump's tweets on Twitter, and later including his weekly rallies – was now going to be President Trump's way of communicating with his supporters. And so, those who followed Q became the Q movement, which today consists of millions of people in the US and in most countries around the globe.

I have personally been reading the Q posts since about mid-2018 and have since published a book on this subject, titled, "President Trump and the Q movement versus Satan and the Deep State." Below are some websites where the Q posts can be found:

https://qalerts.app/

https://qagg.news/

https://qanon.pub/

https://qanon.news/Q/

As to what relates to our present subject, it is through the Q posts that President Trump has let his supporters know the truth about what is really going on in the world, including the C-virus pandemic, which the mainstream media is not reporting the truth about, and which the social media sites, such as Google, YouTube, Tweeter, Facebook, and Instagram, are doing all they can to either hide the truth, or else delete it, including blocking or removing all those seeking to propagate that truth.

It is through the Q posts that President Trump's supporters have had confirmed to them that this so-called 'pandemic' was but a concerted attempt by the Deep State to remove him from office as a primary goal, although as we have seen already, there is a sinister dark agenda being pushed here, which involves bringing in a one world government, including getting everyone on the planet vaccinated, to name but a few. As EXAMPLES ONLY, AND NOT LINKS, please note the Q posts below, with the Q post number and date being given. This is only the tip of the iceberg of information that President Trump and the Q team has been providing supporters:

3909 Democrats Are Determined to Undermine Election Integrity Protections Using C-virus as a Prop
Q!!Hs1Jq13jV6 8 Apr 2020 - 10:02:45 AM
Read in order.
1. https://www.breitbart.com/politics/2020/04/06/gop-gears-up-for-next-

relief-fight-democrats-want-the-federal-government-to-take-over-elections/📁
2. https://www.foxnews.com/opinion/coronavirus-elections-wisconsin-democrats-harmeet-dhillon📁
3. https://twitter.com/realDonaldTrump/status/1247861952736526336📁
Why did WHO make several strong recommendation NOT TO impose a travel ban?
Why did select **[D]** govs ban the use of hydroxychloroquine **[key]**?
Why does FAKE NEWS push anti-hydroxychloroquine **[fear tactics re: use]**?
Why was impeachment pushed through H fast? **[did they count on R's blocking new witnesses?]**
Time sensitive?
Why?
When did **[BIDEN]** become the front runner?
Why was this critically important?
What happened directly after?
WHO BENEFITS THE MOST?
EVERYTHING AT STAKE.
When everything else FAILED….
DO YOU ATTEMPT TO CHEAT?
Welcome to the **[D][People's Republic of China]** party.
The Silent War continues..
[6+]
Q


3918 The Mainstream Media and Democrats Are the Enemy of the People
Q!!Hs1Jq13jV6 9 Apr 2020 - 11:52:31 AM
https://www.foxnews.com/media/ag-william-barr-disappointed-by-partisan-attacks-levied-at-president-trump-says-media-on-a-jihad-against-hydroxychloroquine📁
Difficult to imagine media **[D party]** attempting to squash all hope of a cure?
Difficult to imagine media **[D party]** wanting public to remain in fear **[re C-virus]** up until the election?
Difficult to imagine media **[D party]** willing to sacrifice lives in order to regain power?
ENEMY OF THE PEOPLE.

Difficult truths will soon see the light of day.
Q

3951 **The Out of Shadows Documentary Lifts the Mask on How the CIA, MSM & Hollywood Manipulate the Masses**
Q!!Hs1Jq13jV6 11 Apr 2020 - 10:00:04 PM
https://www.youtube.com/watch?feature=youtu.be&v=MY8Nfzcn1qQ
Best documentary of the year.
[F] black sites are being closed [MK_active]
[CLAS 1-99: future]
Q

4040 **Influenza Deaths Are Being Attributed to C-Virus to Increase Fear/Panic**
Q!!Hs1Jq13jV6 1 May 2020 - 10:40:35 AM
https://www.cdc.gov/nchs/data/health_policy/Provisional-Death-Counts-C-Virus-Pneumonia-and-Influenza.pdf
>11,356 C-virus
>54,217 Pneumonia, Influenza, OR C-virus
Influenza death rate low v previous years?
Knowledge is power.
Information warfare.
Q

4086 **Regular Doctors Using HCQ, Azithromycin and Zinc to Combat C-virus (No Deaths, Quick Recovery)**
Q!!Hs1Jq13jV6 3 May 2020 - 12:42:29 PM
https://twitter.com/DocEvenhouse/status/1256765070245269505
Logical thinking.
Q

4088 **Illinois Releases 146 Sex Offenders, Including 3 'Sexually Dangerous Persons'**
Q!!Hs1Jq13jV6 3 May 2020 - 12:59:42 PM
https://www.mystateline.com/news/local-news/illinois-releases-146-sex-offenders-including-3-sexually-dangerous-persons-convicted-in-winnebago-ogle-counties/
Why are [D] Govs around the Nation releasing convicted felons [dangerous] early?
Why are [D] Govs around the Nation instructing[ed] law enforcement to arrest those who [challenge] do not comply with lockdown order(s)?

Reconcile.
Q

### 4157 We lost 100,000, no shutdown: 1968 Pandemic (H3N2 virus) | Pandemic Influenza (Flu) | CDC
Q!!Hs1Jq13jV6 8 May 2020 - 1:56:34 PM
https://twitter.com/IngrahamAngle/status/1258765736207671297
Is this about the virus OR THE ELECTION?
Q

### 4171 How Is It Possible the Source Country of the Virus (Minus Wuhan) Was on Lockdown for Only 16 Days?
Q!!Hs1Jq13jV6 9 May 2020 - 2:53:07 AM
Origin Country of C-virus: China
Origin City of C-virus: Wuhan
How long was Wuhan on lockdown: 76 days
How long was the remainder of China on lockdown:
CNY extend Jan 24 - Feb 9 (avg): 16 days
https://www.china-briefing.com/news/china-extends-lunar-new-year-holiday-february-2-shanghai-february-9-contain-coronavirus-outbreak/
How long has the US been on lockdown?
No spread of C-virus outside of Wuhan?
How is it possible the source Country of the virus (minus Wuhan) was on lockdown for only 16 days?
How long has the US been on lockdown?
Forecasted lockdown CA, NY, OR, MI, ……?
Reconcile.
Logical thinking.
Q

### 4172 D's Timed Delivery of Impeachment Articles to Draw Attention Away from the 1st US C-virus Infection
Q!!Hs1Jq13jV6 9 May 2020 - 10:53:05 AM
https://www.foxbusiness.com/markets/us-china-sign-historic-trade-deal
Dates are important.
January 15, 2020.
>Historic trade deal w/ China signed
>>China loses billions in clawback

>**[Held][Timed]** impeachment articles are delivered to Senate
>FIRST case of C-virus lands in UNITED STATES **[Seattle-Tacoma International Airport]**
Do the Chinese like losing?
Do the Chinese want POTUS removed/replaced P_elec_2020?
Do the Chinese want BIDEN installed P_elec_2020?
Is this about the virus OR THE ELECTION?
Q


What one also needs to be aware of is that there are hundreds (if not thousands) of websites worldwide that have sprung up since Q started the Q posts, with those owning these websites being decoders or decipherers of the information provided by Q as a help to the general public worldwide, either on a daily basis, or some only when Q posts are posted. For the last two years, I have personally been following the X22 Report, which has a daily Geopolitical and financial report during the week, including Saturdays, plus a key Spotlight interview on Sundays. Below are three episodes from the X22 Report, which have been carefully chosen for the book, as these bring out key information that the reader should be aware of:

X22 Report, Episode 2160b, April 28, 2020:

https://www.youtube.com/watch?v=x_97w-59BDc

X22 Report, Episode 2164b, May 3, 2020:

https://www.youtube.com/watch?v=b4Spym4OVTI

X22 Report, Episode 2171b, May 11, 2020:

https://www.youtube.com/watch?v=pfB1FwOkUNU

But before we close this chapter, we need to revisit the puppet masters that we introduced at the end of Chapter Four, when discussing the Deep State, for there we said we would talk about them again when looking at Q and the Q movement in this chapter. Just to refresh our memories, those puppet masters again are: 1) the House of Saud, in Saudi Arabia; 2) the Rothschild families, in Europe; and 3) George Soros, in the United States (although he operates in almost forty countries through his Open Society Foundation). And so, to begin with here, we only know about these puppet masters due to Q telling us in the Q posts. Please read the following three Q posts very carefully:

## 133 The Puppet Masters
**Q!ITPb.qbhqo 11 Nov 2017 - 9:29:35 PM**
Hard to swallow.
Important to progress.
Who are the puppet masters?
House of Saud (6+++) - $4 Trillion+
Rothschild (6++) - $2 Trillion+
Soros (6+) - $1 Trillion+
Focus on above (3).
Public wealth disclosures – False.
Many governments of the world feed the 'Eye'.
Think slush funds (feeder).
Think war (feeder).
Think environmental pacts (feeder).
Triangle has (3) sides.
Eye of Providence.
Follow the bloodlines.
What is the keystone?
Does Satan exist?
Does the 'thought' of Satan exist?
Who worships Satan?
What is a cult?
Epstein island.
What is a temple?
What occurs in a temple?
Worship?
Why is the temple on top of a mountain?
How many levels might exist below?
What is the significance of the colors, design and symbol above the dome?
Why is this relevant?
Who are the puppet masters?
Have the puppet masters traveled to this island?
When? How often? Why?
"Vladimir Putin: The New World Order Worships Satan"
Q

## 140 Families Combined (TRI) = NWO
**Q!ITPb.qbhqo 11 Nov 2017 - 9:33:51 PM**

Wealth (over generations) buys power.
Power (over generations) buys more wealth/control.
More wealth/control buys countries and its people.
Families combined (TRI) = NWO.
Inner TRI families will collapse.
What is the keystone?
What Nation dominates all others?
What Nation has influence over most others?
What is the keystone?
Return to SA.
Strings cut (+++).
Puppets (+++) in shadows.
Each side of the triangle controls a certain subsect of power brokers.
Power brokers are also labeled as the puppets/servants.
What is the New World Order?
Why did POTUS receive a sword dance when visiting SA?
What does this mean culturally?
Why is this relevant?
What occurred in SA?
How did POTUS remove one side of the pyramid?
What did POTUS receive while visiting China?
Where did POTUS dine?
What is the significance?
What if China, Russia, and others are coordinating w/ POTUS to eliminate the NWO?
Who controls NK?
Who really controls NK?
Who controls several agencies within the US, EU, and abroad?
Why is No Such Agency so vital?
Enormous scale of events currently ongoing.
Why is Russia helping to kill ISIS?
This is not easy to accept nor believe.
Crumbs make bread.
Operations active.
Joint missions underway.
The world is fighting back.
Refer back to graphic.
The Great Awakening.
Snow White.
Iron Eagle.

Jason Bourne (2016)(Dream/CIA).
Q

<u>243</u> **Saudi Arabia Controlled US Politicians**
Q!ITPb.qbhqo 30 Nov 2017 - 10:17:43 PM
SA controlled US puppets.
Strings cut.
D's dropping all around over sexual misconduct (1st stage).
Coincidence directly after SA?
Don't you realize the war has gone public?
List who will not be running for re_election.
Coincidence?
Phase I.
Easy to swallow.
Loss of power/influence.
Good time to prosecute.
Just wait until next week.
You are all Patriots.
Q


Now the reason that these puppet masters were mentioned is that President Trump and his administration need to REMOVE THESE PUPPET MASTERS, since they control whole countries from the top down. And the best way to remove them is by removing their source of funds. And what is critical to realize and grasp here is that President Trump and his administration have used the C-virus pandemic, which they knew in advance through military intelligence and the NSA that it was coming, to do exactly that, and remove the puppet master's sources of funding.

For what we further need to see is that when the WHO declared the coronavirus as a world emergency on January 30th 2020, President Trump declared a national emergency the next day, which then meant that he was from that point on, and which is still ongoing today (May 13, 2020), as a wartime President, with wartime powers. We earlier said that those puppet masters gained much of their wealth through controlling the central bank of almost every country; through the drug trade, and also through the human trafficking trade, including pedophilia rings, which are also operated on a worldwide scale.

So now, while everything was shut down in every country, President Trump and his administration have been busy, through military operations, in dismantling the drug trade and the human trafficking rings worldwide, thereby in effect taking power away from the puppet masters! Again, what is being written here is only known due to following the Q posts. For instance, the US Federal Reserve is no longer part of the Deep State under the Rothschilds, but is now part of the US Treasury Department and reports to Secretary Mnuchin! What this means is that the most important central bank in the world is no longer part of the Deep State, that had formerly been owned and controlled by the Rothschilds. Please see the following very short video on this:

https://www.youtube.com/watch?v=I-ZlgJWihuk

Because the removal of the bad actors worldwide in the human trafficking rings and the drug trade is still ongoing, then Q has not posted much on this, since it is known that the Deep State does read the Q posts. However, below is one Q post from February 6, 2020, which should give us a good idea of the battle taking place behind the scenes, which Q here refers to as 'the silent war,' and which is taking place in the background while this so-called pandemic is ongoing:

3837 **They Tried to Destroy the USA Internally**
Q!!Hs1Jq13jV6 6 Feb 2020 - 9:40:18 PM
BIGGER THAN YOU CAN IMAGINE.
More than selling of State Secrets.
More than selling of US security.
More than selling of MIL tech.
More than selling of C_A assets.
More than selling of NSA bulk data collection programs.
More than selling of Uranium.
More than selling of US Space NAT SEC programs & positions.
More than selling of US AID..
More than selling of SAPs
CLAS 1-99
..................
>Crimes against Humanity.

When you cannot destroy/defeat the United States of America by attacking head on, you change tactics and deploy a 'KILL FROM WITHIN' **[internal]** operation.
>Financial/Economy
>Military/Police
>Division of Citizenry
>Border Collapse
**[Install 'like-minded' leaders in key positions of US Gov]**
How many people **[removed]** from the FBI had Iranian family backgrounds?
The Silent War Continues…..
Q


So as we close this important chapter, please keep in mind that the Deep State, sometimes referred to as the 'swamp' in the Q posts and by President Trump in his tweets, has been entrenched for many years in the federal, state, and local levels, including the judiciary, and health organizations in the US, so that it cannot be removed overnight by President Trump and his administration, although they would like to. And so, people such as Dr Fauci, head of The National Institute of Allergy and Infectious Diseases (NIAID) and Dr Redfield, head of the Centers for Disease Control and Prevention (CDC) are Deep State players, who had to be exposed as such, which President Trump has done while this pandemic has been ongoing. So please keep in mind that he did not appoint these people. It is very important for us to remember that those who are part of the swamp first need to be exposed, along with many others, before he can remove them! And now we also see how important Q and the Q movement really is in holding back Satan's agenda from being carried out on earth at this time!

"Do not let your heart be troubled; believe in God (The Father), believe also in Me (His Son). In My Father's house are many dwelling places; if it were not so, I would have told you; for I go to prepare a place for you. If I go and prepare a place for you, I will come again and receive you to Myself, that where I am, there you may be also."

John 14:11-3

# CHAPTER TEN

## Believers worldwide

Earlier in Chapter Three, we quoted 2 Thessalonians 2:1-12 and there, at verses 6 to 8, we spoke of The Holy Spirit indwelling the believers of earth being the effective restraint to Satan's agenda in the spiritual realm from bringing the antichrist on the world scene. Let us note those verses again here to refresh our memories, including the notes in brackets that were there included as a help, "[6] And you know what restrains him now, so that in his time he (the antichrist) will be revealed. [7] For the mystery of lawlessness is already at work (during this present third age of time); only he (in reference to The Holy Spirit indwelling believers on earth during the present age) who now restrains will do so until he is taken out of the way (when The Holy Spirit is removed from the earth by God, along with all the believers of this present third age, as we see at 1 Thessalonians 4:14-17, then the antichrist will be revealed here on earth, as is clear from the next verse). [8] Then that lawless one (the antichrist) will be revealed whom the Lord (God's Son) will slay with the breath of His mouth and bring to an end by the appearance of His coming (which is now the second stage of His second coming and is at the end of the seven year period, as we see at Revelation 19:11-21)." Since believers, as indwelt of The Holy Spirit, constitute the restraint to Satan carrying out his agenda on earth of bringing in a one world government under the antichrist, then we should not be shocked or surprised to see Satan use the Deep State to seek to eliminate the true believers from the earth!

And there is a very important truth to keep in mind here relating to this, first from a human perspective, and it is the fact that the largest block of support for President Trump in the United States comes from the Evangelical community, which will be key to his re-election in 2020. What that means then, if one is part of the Deep State, is that Evangelical Christians will then become a ready target for all those who are part of that Deep State, whether in the United States or abroad. For in attacking the largest block of supporters that President Trump has, one is in effect preventing him from being re-elected President in 2020!

What is also important to observe is that the majority of those who are part of the Q movement are also believers, and the majority of those who have websites decoding the Q posts, and thereby exposing the Deep State as corrupt and evil, are also believers! Therefore, that provides Satan and the Deep State one more incentive to seek to either eliminate or at least weaken believers through this C-virus pandemic. What this means then is that we should not be surprised that social distancing and quarantining people of faith, which means not being able to gather together, effectively weakens that segment of President Trump's base. One can just shudder to think of what it will be like for believers if any Democrat like Obama comes to the Presidency again!

And then the second very important truth, now from a spiritual perspective, that believers need to keep in mind is that God has made it very clear from Romans 11:25-27 that the present third age of time WILL NOT END until all those who are to come to a personal knowledge of God in salvation through faith in His Son, The Lord Jesus Christ, have been saved! So let us note what God there revealed, "[25] For I do not want you, brethren (speaking to believers of the third age, who were not seeing many come to know God in salvation from among the nation of Israel), to be uninformed of this mystery — so that you will not be wise in your own estimation — that a partial hardening has happened to Israel until the fullness of the Gentiles has come in; [26] and so all Israel will be saved; just as it is written, "The Deliverer (God's Son) will come from Zion (in Heaven), He will remove ungodliness from Jacob (Israel)." [27] This is My (new) covenant with them, when I take away their sins" (through the forgiveness of sins in salvation).

And what God means at verse 25 here, when He says to the believers of the third age of time, "a partial hardening has happened to Israel until the fullness of the Gentiles has come in," is that during the present third age only some of the nation of Israel are being saved by God's mercy, love, and grace; while the rest remain in unbelief, as those who enter the last seven years remaining of the second age of time as the nation of Israel yet in unbelief (which is the majority of them); with the words "until the fullness of the Gentiles has come in" being a reference to the end of the present third age, with the last of those to be saved by God during the third age having now been saved, which is also the resuming point of the second age of time to complete its last seven years. In other words, when God saves the last person of the present third age to be saved out of the nations of the earth, then He ends the third age by bringing each believer to Heaven (noting 1 Thessalonians 4:14-17) as He removes The Holy Spirit from the earth (noting 2 Thessalonians 2:1-7)!

And so, when God's Son returns from Heaven to earth at the end of the seven years remaining of the second age of time, which is after the third age of time, which is in view at verse 25 here, "all Israel will be saved," at that time, in that all the unbelievers of the earth will have died in the seven years of God's judgment on earth during those seven years, leaving only the believers of the nations of the earth, and also the unbelievers of the nation of Israel as yet alive, since these are elect of God unto salvation, as those who are now saved by God's mercy, grace, and love, who now become part of God's new covenant, as we see above at verse 27 of Romans 11. So we can say here that God's number one agenda then is to see a specific number of Gentiles (non-Jews) from the nations of the earth come to faith in His Son before He ends the present third age of time!

What this further means then is that God is not only leaving believers on earth at this time to restrain evil, such as holding back Satan from bringing his evil agenda to earth, but God also wants to use those that are already saved as vessels in His hands to reach those that are yet to come to know God during this third age. As we just saw above, this present third age will not end until all those God has appointed to eternal life (Acts 13:48) are saved!

# CHAPTER ELEVEN

## God Almighty and Sovereign over all

The important questions for us to consider in this chapter are: Why did God allow this man-derived C-virus to be released, then to be called a pandemic, and then for almost cause all activity on earth to cease, which is the first time in recorded history this had ever happened? Since God is Almighty, which means He has all the power that is unlimited; and He is also Sovereign, which means that He has total control over all that exists, then it is clear that God could have prevented these events from occurring, especially since He knew that this had its source with Satan. And so, one obvious answer that comes to those who are believers here is that God is obviously speaking loud and clear, to unbelievers and believers alike!

So the first thing that we all need to realize here is that THINGS WILL NEVER GO BACK TO NORMAL! The door has effectively been closed forever on the world that we knew before this virus was declared a pandemic on March 11, 2020. What this means is that believers especially need to grasp that OUR REDEMPTION DRAWS NEAR, in terms of the return of God's Son from Heaven, our Lord Jesus Christ, to just above the clouds of the earth to remove the believers from the earth, as we see God describe for us at 1 Thessalonians 4:14-17, before starting the last seven years remaining of the second age of time, when God allows Satan to form a one world government and a one world religion, with the antichrist as political leader and the false prophet as religious leader, as we see God describe for us at Revelation 6:1 to 17-18.

So what this means is that God is making us aware through this unprecedented event that THE TIME IS SHORT, so that unbelievers need to get right with God, and believers need to be living for God in order to be available vessels in His Hands to reach those among the unbelievers that are turning to Him!

And so, my prayer is that we all now have, as believers, a heightened awareness that we are indeed living in the last days of this present age. And in now having this awareness this should not leave us the same as before one started reading this book. Hopefully, it has led one to ask, "How am I to live then, in the light of the fact that we are in the last days?"

In answer to that, we need to be aware of what God says we need to do when we realize we are living in times such as these, noting now what we read at Ephesians 5:15-17, "[15] Therefore be careful how you walk, not as unwise men but as wise, [16] MAKING THE MOST OF YOUR TIME, BECAUSE THE DAYS ARE EVIL. [17] So then do not be foolish, but understand what the will of the Lord is." From this quote from God's word to us we see that God here asks three things of us "because the days are evil." The first thing that God wants those who have a personal relationship with Him to do then is to be careful how we walk as children of God yet on earth.

If we know that this world is a dark place, then we are to walk in the light as God is in the light, noting what we read at 1 John 1:5-7, "[5] This is the message we have heard from Him and announce to you, that God is Light, and in Him there is no darkness at all. [6] If we say that we have fellowship with Him and yet walk in the darkness, we lie and do not practice the truth; [7] but if we walk in the Light as He Himself is in the Light, we have fellowship with one another, and the blood of Jesus His Son cleanses us from all sin."

To walk with God in the light here requires that we walk with Him with NO KNOWN UNCONFESSED SINS IN OUR LIVES. So the first thing we can do each day is to have a quiet time with God for the purpose of examining ourselves before Him to ensure that we have no unconfessed sins in our lives, by asking God to point out any sins in our lives, and then to confess those sins to Him as He points them out, doing so in accordance with 1 John 1:9, which is the only confessional God provided for those who are His, "If we confess our sins, He is faithful and righteous to forgive us our sins and to cleanse us from all unrighteousness."

Then once we are walking with God in the light as He is in the light, we are ready to face the day and people we encounter in the light of what He then tells us to do, noting now what we read at Philippians 2:14-16, "[14] Do all things without grumbling or disputing; [15] so that you will PROVE YOURSELVES TO BE BLAMELESS AND INNOCENT, CHILDREN OF GOD ABOVE REPROACH IN THE MIDST OF A CROOKED AND PERVERSE GENERATION, among whom you appear as lights in the world, [16] holding fast the word of life, so that in the day of Christ I will have reason to glory because I did not run in vain nor toil in vain."

People around us will then be aware that we are children of God, as cleansed of known sins and available vessels in which God dwells, so that by His grace and His power working in us we can minister the word of God, which can bring life to a lost world. Notice that God does not want us to do as the world does here, which is to complain and argue, but rather we are to prove to be "children of God above reproach in the midst of a crooked and perverse generation." Let us make a difference for God while here!

Then please note from Ephesians 5:15-17 quoted above that the second thing that God wants us to do in light of these evil times we live in is to make the most of our time each day, which requires wisdom from God, for we do not know how to live in a way that will count for eternity! In other words, when we are in that quiet time with God first thing each morning, we can ask Him to guide us through the day ahead of us so that the day may be outworked in such a way as to count for eternity. God always answers such requests. We are each given only a certain amount of time on earth by God. Let us then use our brief time here on earth wisely, being guided by God in our daily walk in this present world.

And then the third thing which God would have us do in the light of our being in the last days of this present age is to be aware of what GOD'S WILL is moment by moment so as to live each day in the will of God for our lives. We need to be aware that we have been saved in order to serve God while here on earth, which means seeking to carry out His will in this world and not our own! Therefore, when we are with Him in that quiet time first thing in the morning, we can also say to Him, "Your will be done this day and not my own," and then ask Him to guide us into all His will for the day ahead of us. That too is one request that God will surely fulfill, guaranteed!

For what needs to also be grasped here is what God's own precious Son said to His Father while on earth at His first coming from Heaven to earth, noting what we now read at John 6:38, "For I have come down from heaven, not to do My own will, but the will of Him who sent Me." At His first coming, God's Son lived on earth as a Pattern for us on how to live while here for the glory of God. He was here to pay the penalty due sin on our behalf, which is death. God does not want us to die physically each day, but He does want us to die to our self-will that we might live for the will of God! We will be passing through this life on earth only once, so let us make it count for eternity!

And so, as we close this chapter, my prayer for all those who are believers is what God says at Luke 1:74,75, "To grant us that we, being rescued from the hand of our enemies, might serve Him without fear, in holiness and righteousness before Him all our days." Amen, amen, and amen.

"I have given them your word; and the world has hated them, because they are not of the world, even as I am not of the world."

John 17:14

# CHAPTER TWELVE

## A last word

There are two realities that should be mentioned as we close. The first is that I am now a few months into my 70$^{th}$ year. And although I am relatively healthy and have no preconditions (that I know of), nevertheless, I fall in the category of seniors, and it is seniors that the C-virus has been mainly taking out. What I am getting at here is that a lot of the information that I have received over my lifetime have come from the older generation, either in person, from books, magazine articles, or on the internet. What this means is that in Satan bringing this man-made virus to wreak destruction on nations worldwide through the Deep State of earth, it has taken out many of that older generation, who no doubt were and are helping the younger generations navigate through this life by means of their accumulated wisdom and knowledge. This is certainly not something that the devil is ignorant of, which therefore means that it is no coincidence, but rather part of Satan's sinister plan to take out the older generation, which then makes it that much easier for his agenda to be implemented!

The second reality that should be mentioned is that with each passing year, we seem to be seeing fewer and fewer critical thinkers! And by a critical thinker here, I mean someone who is able to analyze data and facts and come to an objective conclusion based on the evidence, irrespective of what the prevailing 'group think' might be saying. In other words, someone who is still able to think for one's self!

While reading one of the local papers this evening, what struck me, as I read the news of what is taking place here, relative to this pandemic, is that I felt like an alien that just landed here, with no connection whatsoever with the collective group think that is so prevalent, even locally! Or to put it another way, it is as if I was living in a parallel universe than those around me. And even though this is now May 24, 2020, as this is being written, nevertheless, health authorities are saying that everything might be closed down until fall. Dear God, that is almost six months away! Are there no rational thinkers left that realize as I do that these people have gone stark naked insane! Do they not have their eyes open to see the truth?

And of course, the only answer to that is that they are not insane, but only blinded to the truth, simply because they are being conditioned to accept the devil's lies, so as to be totally prepared to accept the antichrist as he comes on the world scene, which event could occur at any time. Let us notice what God tells us at 2 Thessalonians 2:9-12, [9] that is, the one (the antichrist) whose coming is in accord with the activity of Satan, with all power and signs and false wonders, [10] and with all the deception of wickedness for those who perish, because they (the unbelievers of the present age) did not receive the love of the truth so as to be saved. [11] For this reason God will send upon them (the unbelievers) a deluding influence so that THEY WILL BELIEVE WHAT IS FALSE (because already totally conditioned to believe lies, such as fake news!), [12] in order that they all may be judged who did not believe the truth, but took pleasure in wickedness." "

**To God alone be all praise, honor, and glory, with thanksgiving, both now and forevermore! Amen, amen, and amen.**

# ADDENDUM A

## / The four ages of time

What is important to know when reading God's word, the Bible, is that God has divided time into four ages. And since God's word covers all of time, then all of God's word, the Bible, can be subdivided along the lines of these four ages. But before noting what these four ages are, we need to also be aware that in each of the four ages of time, God uses the believers of that age as His vessels. In other words, God is accomplishing His work on earth through the believers of each age of time. And what is also important to keep in mind in regards to this is that although God starts each age with believers, before long the number of unbelievers in each age outnumbers the number of believers. In other words, one characteristic of each age of time is that there is a believing remnant among a mass of unbelievers, with these believers in each age being those whom God preserves for Himself and through whom God works to accomplish His purposes in each age through time.

And so, in THE FIRST AGE OF TIME, God worked through Adam and his believing descendants as His vessels to accomplish His will on earth, which age covers the first eleven chapters of Genesis. What this means is that they were the believers who willingly served Him out of love for Him. In other words, this was the believing line of descent, or the believing remnant, through which God worked out His will. Then when we begin Genesis 12, we see God take one believer, Abraham, and out of that one man's descendants through the line of Isaac, and then through the line of Jacob, God makes a nation, which is Israel. And again, we need to see that only the believing line of descent within the nation of Israel was the remnant through which God worked to accomplish His will. What this means is that not all those who were of the nation of Israel were believers. In fact, the majority were unbelievers. Therefore, in THE SECOND AGE OF TIME, which goes from Genesis 12 to the end of Malachi in the Old Testament, and includes the gospel accounts of Matthew, Mark, Luke, and John, plus Acts 1 and Revelation 6 to 19 in the New Testament, God works out His will in time through the believers of the nation of Israel, which is again a small number compared to the total number.

And here we need to pause for a moment and mention something else before going on to consider the third age of time, and this is the fact of representation. What this means is that in the first age of time, we have Adam and Eve as our first parents, who were but representative of all people on earth. In other words, God knew that what this one couple did, any other couple would have done the same thing had they been in their place, since God knows that once sin entered His perfect and sinless creation, we all would have the same sinful nature as human beings.

Then the same is true in regards to the nation of Israel in the second age of time, in that God knew that what this one nation did, any other nation on earth would likewise have done had it been chosen by God as a representative nation. So when God set out to make the one nation of Israel, He started out with just believers. But when the nation of Israel came into existence later, only a believing remnant within the nation were believers. Now since the nation of Israel was but representative of all the nations, then God knew that if He had chosen any other nation on earth, He would find that only a believing remnant would ever become believers to serve Him willingly out of love for Him out of a mass of unbelievers who would not in any of those nations also. In other words, no other human being would have acted any differently than our first parents, and likewise, no other nation would have acted any differently than the nation of Israel did. This means that all human beings and all nations are likewise guilty before God.

What also needs to be mentioned here as we now go on to look at the third age of time, is that the first two ages basically cover the time period covered by the Old Testament, which means that the remaining third and fourth ages of time must be covered by the New Testament portion of God's word, the Bible. And let us recall that in the first age, God worked through the believers of that age, beginning with Adam, while in the second age of time, God worked through the believers of the nation of Israel, beginning with Abraham. So as we come to THE THIRD AGE OF TIME, which goes from Acts 2 to the end of Revelation 5 in God's word, the Bible, we have God working through the believers of earth, whom God calls "the church."

What this means then is that in this third age of time, which we are presently still in, God is accomplishing His will through all the believers of earth, with God now not looking at any specific nation in particular. In other words, during the present third age of time, also known as the church age, the nation of Israel, although being supernaturally preserved by God, is still just the same as any other nation on earth, having a believing remnant among a majority of unbelievers.

Then in THE FOURTH AGE OF TIME, which is basically covered by Revelation 20 to 22 in the New Testament, although mentioned often in prophecy in various portions of the Old Testament, we have God working through the believers of that age, but now with much greater variation. In other words, during the fourth age of time God works through the believers of every nation on earth still in their natural bodies, and also through the believers of the first three ages of time, who would have experienced their part in the first resurrection relating to believers and who are now in their resurrected bodies. This is covered in much greater detail in my book, "An Introduction To The New World That Is Coming Upon The Earth," which focuses on this fourth age of time. If there are any readers who are not sure of what is meant by the first and second resurrection and the fact of people serving God in their new resurrected bodies in the future, please see my book, "Have You Ever Wondered What Happens After Death?"

Before leaving this Addendum, it is also important to be aware that the Old Testament portion of God's word, the Bible, contains 39 books, which deal with THE BEGINNING OF ALL THINGS in God's plan of the ages, while the New Testament portion of God's word, the Bible, contains 27 books, which deal with THE CONSUMMATION OF ALL THINGS in God's eternal plan, which God is outworking through the four ages of time. Also of great value is knowing that the second age of time is not completed until AFTER the completion of the all unbelievers of earth of the present time, before establishing His reign on earth as King during the fourth age of time. This is again disclosed by God in many portions of God's word in the New Testament, but especially in passages such as Matthew 24:29,30 and Revelation 19:11-21. Therefore, as we next turn to look at the subject matter of this book proper it is good to remember all that we have just looked at in Addendum A and B as background information and as a foundation for what we are now going to look at in the book.

"Jesus said to him, "I am the way, and the truth, and the life; no one comes to the Father but through Me." "

John 14:6

## ADDENDUM C

## / For those who may not as yet know God

Possibly you have been reading this book and have become aware of not yet knowing this God Who created us and gave us physical life into this world, and up to now has allowed you to live on earth. However, you do have the desire to know God in a personal way. If this is the case, then this chapter has been written specifically for you. And what God wants you to have in coming to know Him is the peace and joy which comes in knowing that all of your sins committed in your lifetime are forgiven and that you have eternal life with God. And so, your greatest need at the moment is to make peace with God so as to go to Heaven, which is God's eternal home. And so, this chapter will help to bring that about by pointing you to God so as to come to faith in His Son.

And as we begin, we need to note a most important promise which God makes at Romans 6:23 to all those who do not yet know Him, "For the wages of sin is death, but the free gift of God is eternal life in Christ Jesus our Lord." The good news here is that God offers you eternal life with Him as a free gift, which is to be obtained in His Son, Jesus Christ. What God does not do in this verse from the Bible is tell us how to obtain that eternal life with Him. Another verse which we can look at where God does let us know how one can obtain that eternal life with Him is noting what God tells us at John 3:16, "For God so loved the world, that He gave His only begotten Son, that whoever believes in Him shall not perish, but have eternal life." Now the added truth which God makes known here is that the eternal life, which He gives to a human being as a free gift, is for those who believe in His Son.

Then the question is: What is it that I am to believe about God's Son, Jesus Christ, which will lead God to give me eternal life with Him forever? And the beauty of God is that He never leaves us guessing, especially when it comes to having a personal relationship with Him, which He desires us to have. Therefore, we should not be surprised when God gives us the answer to our question in what He tells us at 1 Corinthians 15:1-4, "[1] Now I make known to you, brethren, the gospel which I preached to you, which also you received, in which also you stand, [2] by which also you are saved, if you hold fast the word which I preached to you, unless you believed in vain. [3] For I delivered to you as of first importance what I also received, that Christ died for our sins according to the Scriptures, [4] and that He was buried, and that He was raised on the third day according to the Scriptures..." Therefore, "the gospel," which simply means 'good news,' which God wants you to hear and believe in order to "be saved," which simply refers to you coming to know God and have eternal life with Him, is that His Son has already died for you, has already been buried, and has already been raised from the dead again the third day after His death, in order that God would have a basis by which to forgive you of all your sins, which are all against Him, and to freely give you eternal life with Him, for simply believing this message in your heart.

One thing which often prevents a person from believing the gospel at this point is not seeing oneself as a sinner before a Holy God. When we look at ourselves by our own assessment, and especially when we compare ourselves with others around us, we often think of ourselves as being better than others, and so good enough to enter Heaven in our present condition. The problem with this is that it is the product of our own thinking and is not God's assessment of our situation. God's assessment of our situation is as He tells us at Romans 3:10-12,23 in part, "[10] as it is written, "There is none righteous, not even one... [11] there is none who seeks for God [12] all have turned aside... there is none who does good, there is not even one... [23] for all have sinned and fall short of the glory of God..." Quite a different assessment of the human race from that which we as human beings often have of ourselves, is this not? But why would God have such an assessment of the whole human race? For the answer to that question, we need to be aware that God is Creator of all that exists, so that when God created the first man, Adam, at the beginning of time, God created him in innocence, meaning that Adam as first created by God neither knew good nor evil, nor was there any sin anywhere in God's original sinless creation.

However, the day came when God tested Adam with a command, saying to him in the garden of Eden here on earth, which was the perfect environment which God had for him, what we now read at Genesis 2:16,17, "The Lord God commanded the man, saying, "From any tree of the garden you may eat freely; [17] but from the tree of the knowledge of good and evil you shall not eat, for in the day that you eat from it you will surely die." How important to see here that God gave Adam, who although a real person was also representative of the whole human race, the warning of the penalty of death for disobedience to His command.

Unfortunately, the day did come when Adam did partake of the forbidden tree and thereby did sin against God. The moment that happened, Adam not only became a sinner by practice, but also a sinner by nature. One thing my parents had to continually do while under their care was to restrain me from continually going the wrong way, for it seemed that of myself I could not do good, but kept going into sin. The reason this was happening is that from the age of accountability onwards, I had not only become a sinner by practice, but also a sinner by nature. And here the age of accountability needs to be seen as being when as a young child in innocence - which moment is known only by God - one comes to learn the right from the wrong and chooses the wrong, thereby becoming personally accountable to God for one's own sin against Him, since all sin is first of all against Him. And that is why God can say at Romans 3:23 above that "all have sinned and fall short of the glory of God," because God knows that all human beings will go the way of Adam, our representative man, which is also why God can say what He does in regards to the whole of the human race at Romans 5:12, where we read, "Therefore, just as through one man (Adam) sin entered into the world, and death through sin, and so death spread to all men, because all sinned" (from the age of accountability onward).

And so, we see that the whole human race is declared by God to not only be sinners by practice and by nature from the age of accountability onwards, but the whole of the human race is now subject to death! In other words, in God's sight the whole of the human race is under the judgment of the penalty of death, due to all being sinners by practice and by nature. You will recall above, in the first verse we quoted from Romans 6:23, God did say there that "the wages of sin is death." And what God means by "death" here is not just loss of physical life, when the physical body we have dies, but also has spiritual death in mind, which is far worse! Spiritual death has its beginning when a separation takes place between a person and God at the moment one becomes a sinner at the age of accountability and ends after the final judgment of time, when God forever casts away from His Presence those who before physical death refused to believe in His Son, Jesus Christ, thereby personally forfeiting the forgiveness of their sins and eternal life with God. And now all such will pay the penalty for their own sins in hell, away from the Presence of God forever.

It is in the midst of such a hopeless situation in which the whole of the human race found itself in that God TOOK THE INITIATIVE and sent His own eternally existing Son into the world, as born of a virgin in the innocence of Adam – so as not to inherit the sinful nature passed on from generation after generation from Adam onwards – so that He might be the acceptable sacrifice offered to God His Father at the cross, there bearing our sins in His body, and there dying the death due our sins! God's Son, Jesus Christ, was then buried and raised from the dead the third day, to ever be alive, for it is through Him, on the basis of what God has done for us through His Son, that God The Father forgives our sins and imparts us eternal life.

Now, by God's grace and His enablement, may you see your need of God's Son to be Your Savior from the penalty due sin, which is death, not only physical, but also spiritual. And by God's grace, may He lead you to believe in His Son, Jesus Christ, and in believing, to receive the forgiveness of your sins and eternal life with Him forever! And based on the truth just shared, the author would now like to ask you a few questions, with the answer being just between yourself and God:

When God says at Romans 3:23, "for all have sinned and fall short of the glory of God," does that include you?

When God says at Romans 5:8, "But God demonstrates His own love toward us, in that while we were yet sinners, Christ died for us," were you included in Christ's death on behalf of sinners?

And when God further says at 1 Peter 3:18 in part, "For Christ also died for sins once for all, the just for the unjust, so that He might bring us to God, having been put to death in the flesh, but made alive in the spirit," were you part of the unjust for whom Christ died?

When God says at Romans 6:23, "For the wages of sin is death, but the free gift of God is eternal life in Christ Jesus our Lord," do you want that eternal life as a free gift from God?

When God says at John 3:16, "For God so loved the world, that He gave His only begotten Son, that whoever believes in Him shall not perish, but have eternal life," do you now believe that Jesus Christ is indeed God's Son in human flesh, Who came from Heaven to this earth to die in your place, so as to save you from ever experiencing the judgment of God leading to an eternal separation from God in hell?

And when God then further says to you at Isaiah 55:6, "Seek the Lord while He may be found; call upon Him while He is near," for His further promise to you here is as we read at Romans 10:9-11,13, "[9] that if you confess with your mouth Jesus as Lord, and believe in your heart that God raised Him from the dead, you will be saved (that is, you will now enter into a personal relationship with God by faith); [10] for with the heart a person believes, resulting in righteousness (that is, in now receiving God's own righteous life to live by), and with the mouth he confesses, resulting in salvation (that is, in now receiving as a free gift the forgiveness of sins and eternal life with God). [11] For the Scripture says, "Whoever believes in Him will not be disappointed..." [13] for "Whoever will call on the name of the Lord will be saved." Will you now call upon God from your heart, telling God in your own words your answer to each question that has just been asked?

The author's prayer for you at this point, as you now call upon God by His grace, is what we read at Romans 15:13, "Now may the God of hope fill you with all joy and peace in believing, so that you will abound in hope by the power of the Holy Spirit."

# ADDENDUM D

# / Useful Resources

Please note that all video links were active at the time the book was published. If for some reason a link is not active – which could be because a video has been removed by YouTube, for example – then please do a search on one of the following conservative and uncensored alternative sites that have sprung up:

https://www.bitchute.com/

https://www.altcensored.com/

https://drop.space/

And one final note to the reader here, which is that Amazon blocked my book from publication. After an appeal, I was only allowed to have the book published on their platform if I removed all references to this virus from the book. This necessitated my going through the book and inserting C-virus for the official name given by the WHO to this virus, including in the Q posts given as examples.

# / The next book

As this book is being published, the next book that God has given His approval to is, "God's Second Letter Through Peter," which would be the twelfth book in The Word Of God Library series, and the author's fifty-fourth published work. But in case it is not the book that is written, readers may want to stay current with the author's main website, where it will be made known if another book has been written. My main website is:

http://www.pilgrimpathwaypublications.com

And if you have enjoyed reading this book or any other of the author's books, please feel free to give me feedback at the above website, and also let family, friends, and co-workers know about this book and my other books. The author is not on any social media sites, so he relies on God and readers like you to spread the word. May God bless you for doing so!

Printed in Great Britain
by Amazon